KING GEORGE COUNTY HISTORICAL SOCIETY thanks **Union Bank & Trust** for its financial, as well as moral, support. Without their help, this book would have been impossible.

We would also like to thank others who have supported our efforts in this endeavor:

Somerset Homes
Birchwood Power Partners, LP
BB&T Bank

And to our contributing writers:

Tripp Wiggins
Sue Williams
Bill Deyo

To the many who took the time to dig into attics and old photo albums, and our proofreaders who kept us in line.

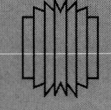

THE
DONNING COMPANY
PUBLISHERS

King George County

A PICTORIAL HISTORY

Elizabeth Nuckols Lee
Jean Moore Graham

Copyright © 2006 by the King George County Historical Society
Second printing 2007

All rights reserved, including the right to reproduce this work in any form whatsoever without permission in writing from the publishers, except for brief passages in connection with a review. For information, write:

The Donning Company Publishers
184 Business Park Drive, Suite 206
Virginia Beach, VA 23462–6533

Steve Mull, General Manager
Barbara Buchanan, Office Manager
Jamie R. Watson, Editor
Amy Thomann, Graphic Designer
Mellanie Denny, Imaging Artist
Scott Rule, Director of Marketing
Stephanie Linneman, Marketing Coordinator
Lori Porter, Project Research Coordinator

Dennis Walton, Project Director

Library of Congress Cataloging-in-Publication Data

Lee, Elizabeth Nuckols.
  King George County, Virginia : a pictorial history / by Elizabeth Nuckols Lee and Jean Moore Graham.
    p. cm.
  Includes bibliographical references and index.
  ISBN-13: 978-1-57864-383-7 (hardcover : alk. paper)
  ISBN-10: 1-57864-383-X (hardcover : alk. paper)
 1. King George County (Va.)--History. 2. King George County (Va.)--History--Pictorial works. I. Graham, Jean Moore, 1936- II. Title.
  F232.K45L438 2006
  975.5'25--dc22
                                2006031815

Printed in the United States of America by Walsworth Publishing Company

Dedication

To the citizens of King George County, Virginia, past and present, who have given of their time, their wealth, and their lives to serve, protect, defend, and ensure prosperity within our community since 1720. And to our children and grandchildren, that they may know and take pride in their heritage.

Table of Contents

8   FOREWORD

9   PREFACE

10   CHAPTER 1: In the Beginning...
- The American Indians
- The First Settlers
- The Maryland–Virginia Boundary Established
- Northern Neck Proprietary
- King George I
- Formation of King George County
- Boundary Changes

20   CHAPTER 2: County Government
- The Courthouse
- County Seal
- Fire Department
- Rescue Squad
- Telephone Service
- Lewis Egerton Smoot Library
- Barnesfield Park
- Wayside Park
- Community Organizations

32   CHAPTER 3: People Who Left Their Mark
- George Washington
- James Madison
- Joseph Jones
- William "Extra Billy" Smith
- Thomas Lomax Hunter
- Thomas Benton Gayle
- Carolinus Peyton
- James Monroe
- John Wilkes Booth: A Visitor of Note

44   CHAPTER 4: Making a Living
- Bristol Iron Works
- Robert Walker
- Canneries
- Mills
- Vulcan Brick Company
- The Local Store
- Hotels and Motels
- Dairies
- The Circle
- The Navy Moves In
- Post Offices

66   CHAPTER 5: When Duty Calls
        Revolutionary War
        War of 1812
        Mexican War
        King George County Survives the War Between the States
        Spanish-American War
        World War I
        World War II
        Korea
        Vietnam
        Iraq

78   CHAPTER 6: Places in Our Hearts

110 CHAPTER 7: We Worship
        The Baptist Church
        The Methodist Church
        The Lutheran Church
        The Catholic Church

124 CHAPTER 8: We Learn
        Schools During the War Between the States
        Rosenwald Schools
        The School Grows
        Elementary Schools
        High Schools
        Middle School
        Superintendent of Schools

138 CHAPTER 9: Transportation and Waterways
        Waterways: Early Transportation Routes
            The Potomac River
            Machodoc Creek
            Rosier's Creek
            The Rappahannock River
        Travel by Land
        Railroad

160 CHAPTER 10: Unforgettable Events
        Leedstown Resolutions
        King George County Fair
        The James Madison Bridge Opening
        The Morgantown Bridge Opening
        Gambling on the Potomac
        Fall Festival
        The Fire of 1963
        Bicentennial Wagon Train Stop
        Today

170 BIBLIOGRAPHY
171 INDEX
176 ABOUT THE AUTHORS

Foreword

In July 2005, King George County was named the best small town in the southeastern section of the United States by American City Business Journals. The ranking took into account income, value of owner-occupied homes, and racial diversity.

This came as no surprise to the residents of the county who had been here for many years. King George County is ideally located away from the metropolitan area of Northern Virginia, yet is close enough to Richmond, Virginia, and to Washington, D.C., to consider them a local drive. The two rivers to the north and south of the county provide water activities. King George remains a rural community, yet has a major defense facility to boost its economy. The farmer and the scientist live as neighbors.

Situated in the Northern Neck, King George County sons were intimately involved in the colonization of the New World and in the creation of our nation. Our roads have been trod by such countrymen as George Washington, James Monroe, the Lees, the Carters, and the Fitzhughs.

Although still mostly rural, King George County's population continues to grow. However, it still maintains a small-town way of life that most residents seem to enjoy.

Preface

As modernizations such as subdivisions, supermarkets, fast foods, and multilane highways become a part of our way of life, it has become increasingly important to preserve for our children and grandchildren the knowledge of life as it was for our parents and grandparents. Life was not always ideal for our community. We cannot, nor do we desire to, change our past. But we intend to be true to our history—for history must not only reflect pride in our heritage, but it must reflect those inhumanities and blunders from which we must learn. We are who we are because of what our ancestors did or did not do. Young people, especially today, need to know and understand how hard our forefathers labored to make life for us what we have now. For only by understanding can they make life better for their children and grandchildren.

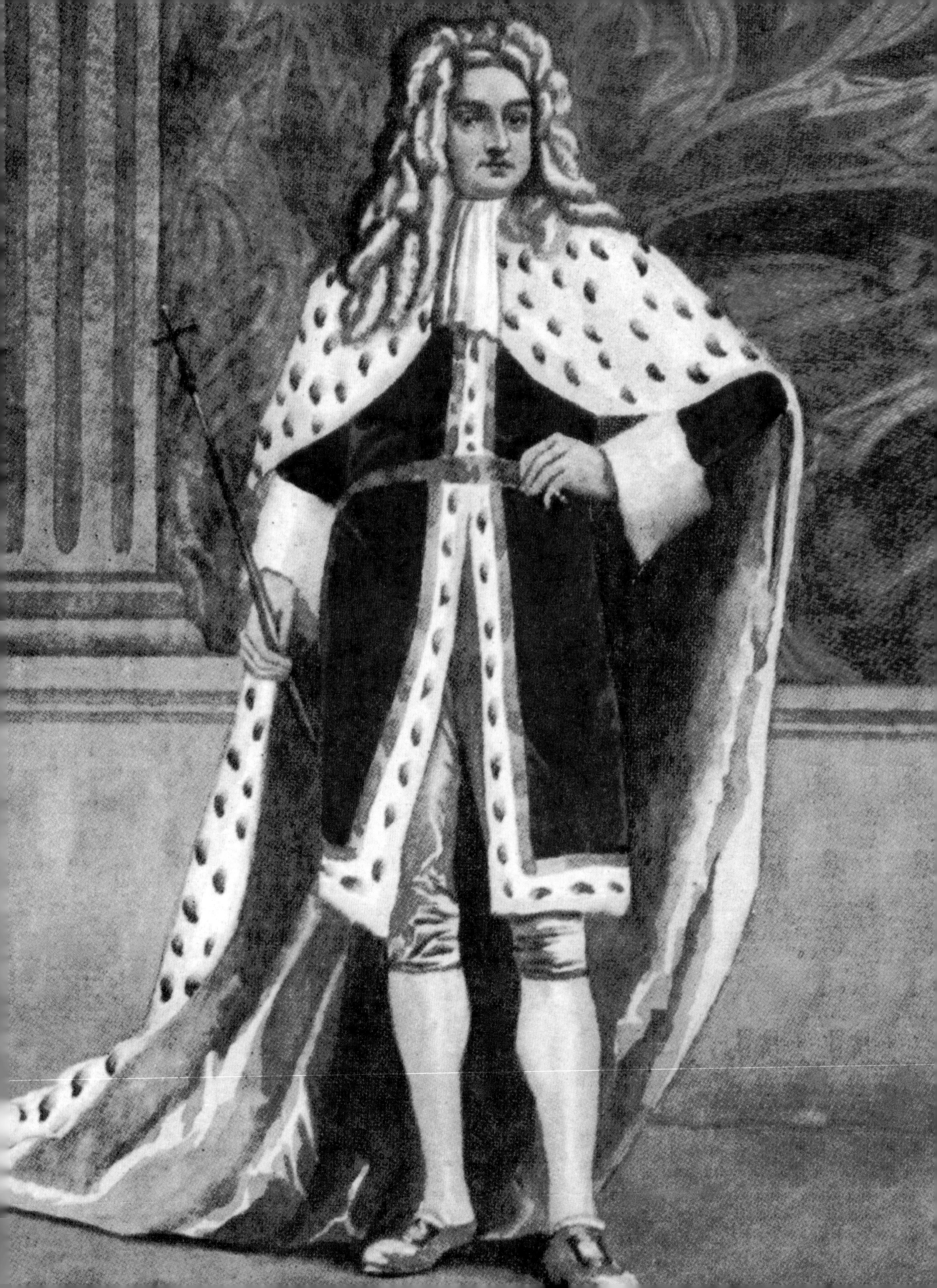

CHAPTER 1
In the Beginning...

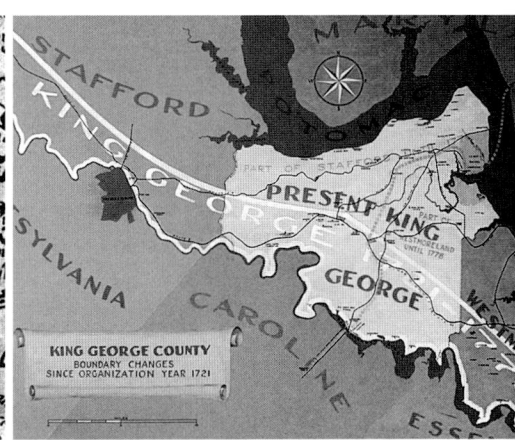

— THE AMERICAN INDIANS —

Indians plied both the Potomac and Rappahannock rivers for countless generations before the arrival of white settlers. Historians say that people lived in Virginia for more than ten thousand years before European contact. Fossils of giant oysters on both the Potomac and Rappahannock rivers have been found in King George, signifying a bounty of food. John Smith explored the Chesapeake Bay in 1608. Among his travels, he visited the area and recorded several American Indian villages. He recorded, "Heaven & earth never agreed better to frame a place for man's habitation; were it fully matured and inhabited by industrious people. Here are mountaines, hils, plaines, valleys, rivers, and brookes, all running most pleasantly into a fair Bay, compassed but for the mouth, with fruitfull and delightsome land."

When the English and Africans began arriving, most of the coastal plain was occupied by Iroquoians, collectively known as Powhatan. Indian villages were scattered along forested shores where inhabitants gathered oysters, fished, and hunted wild fowl from their log canoes. There was no need to travel far inland to hunt because deer, other animals, and water were plentiful along the shores.

Captain John Smith wrote, "Their houses are built like our arbors of small young sprigs, bowed and tied, and so close covered with mats or the bark of trees very handsomely, that with strong wind, rain, or as warm as stoves, but very smokey, yet at the top of the house there is a hole made for the smoke to go into right over the fire. They were oblong with a rounded roof. They were from 12 to 24 yards through and not very wide." The Indians cultivated land bordering the rivers, growing corn, beans, and pumpkins. The rivers served as a highway as they traveled from one settlement to another using dugout canoes.

According to John Reed Swanton's *The Indian Tribes of North America*, the Powhatan tribe had several subtribes that lived in the present-day King George area. The Patawomeck tribe was once a very large tribe with a number of villages in the area of Potomac Creek. The village of the lesser chief, I-Opassus, or Japasaw as he was called by the English, was in the area of Passapatanzy. Japasaw was often referred to as "Chief Passapatanzy." His son, Chief Wahaganoche, also lived in the same area and left descendants, many of whom are part of the present-day Patawomeck tribe. Even though most of the Patawomeck descendants are now concentrated in the White Oak area of Stafford County, a large number of descendants currently live in King George County. The Patawomeck tribe was friendly toward the settlers of Jamestown and helped them to survive by providing them with corn and other food. Even though the tribe was related by blood to the Pamunkeys, they refused to take part in the 1622 massacre against the English settlers. Notable descendants of the Patawomeck tribe include former president Harry S. Truman and singer Wayne Newton.

The *Cuttatawomen* were located near Lamb's Creek on the Rappahannock River. Local subtribes consisted of a number of villages, including the *Sockobeck* site in the Lamb's Creek area. According

Fossils found on the Potomac River. *King George County Museum*

Giant oyster shells, approximately six inches across, found near the Potomac River, are believed to be millions of years old. Similar oysters were found on the Rappahannock River. *King George County Museum*

to John Smith's map, the *Kerahocaks* settled on the north bank of the Rappahannock River, several miles above the *Pissaseck*. This area is also known as Greenlaw's Wharf. Nanzemund or Nanzemond Town was located near Millbank Creek. In Frank Speck's *Rappahannock Indians of Virginia*, he states that the Toppahanocks, also known as the Rappahannocks, had a settlement above the Cuttatawomen on the north side of the Rappahannock River. About two miles above Taliaferro's Mount, the Rappahannock River makes a wide bend eastward. Near here is Dogue Run, named after the *Doeg* tribe, thought to have come from Maryland. The Dogue/Doeg tribal name is found in several early Maryland land grants and surveys. Some researchers believe the tribe was part of the Nanticokes on the Eastern Shore. A 1673 map by Augustine Herrman shows "Doogs Indian Town" located on the Rappahannock. According to David I. Bushnell's *Indian Sites Below the Falls of the Rappahannock, Virginia*, the identity of the Dogue/Doeg Indians has not been clearly determined. Hough Creek enters the Rappahannock about one mile above Dogue Run. Although no named villages are indicated on early maps, many artifacts have been found in this area, including projectile points, bits of pottery, and soapstone fragments. These findings suggest that there was likely a settlement in that area prior to the coming of the English in 1608. At the mouth of Millbank Creek, on the north bank of the Rappahannock about five miles from Chingoteague Creek, archaeologists discovered a Folsom point, a rare arrow-shaped implement. Pottery shards found in this same area depict a variety of decorative methods used by local Indians.

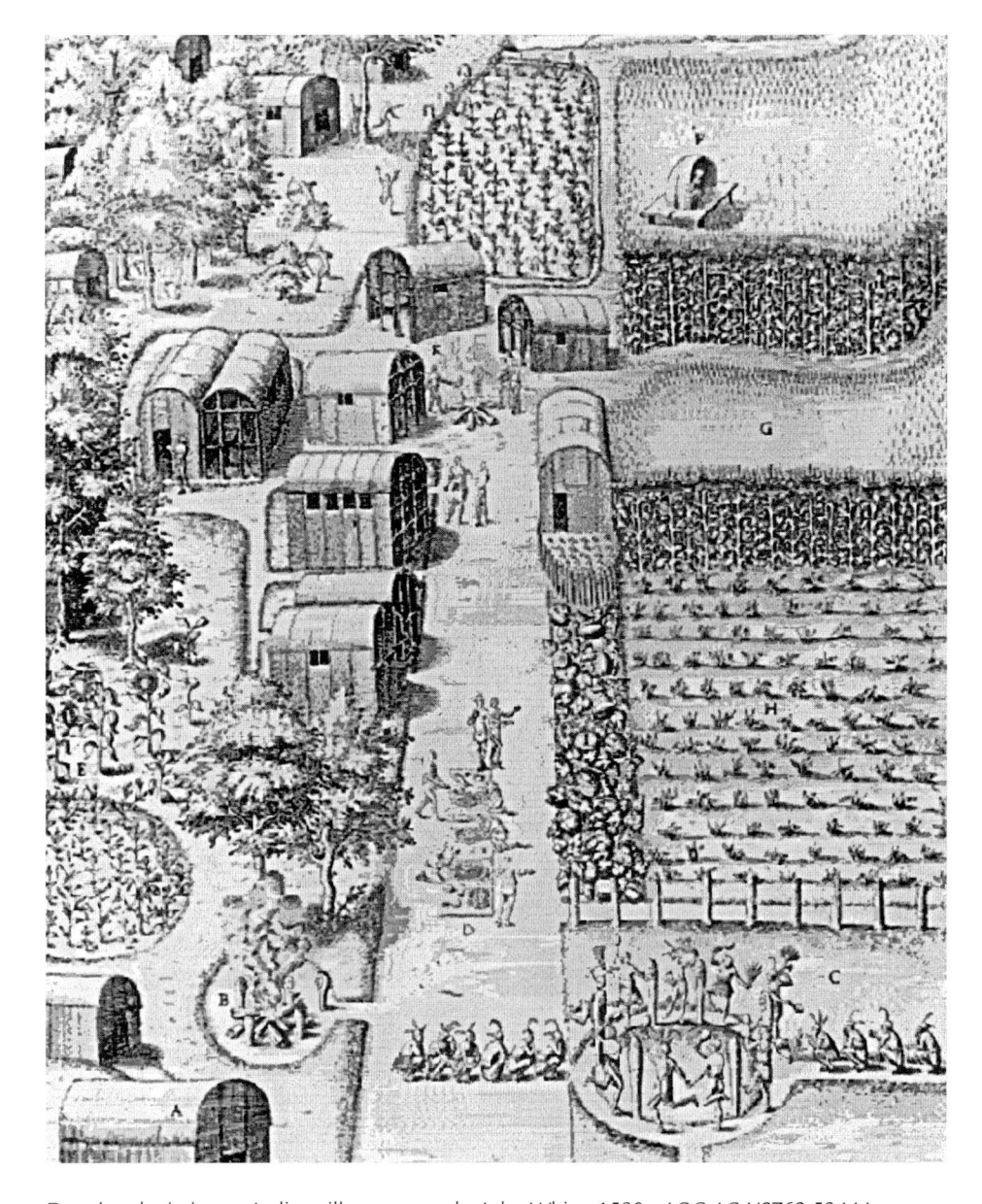

Drawing depicting an Indian village as seen by John White, 1580s. *LOC, LC-USZ62-52444*

The map, created by Captain John Smith in 1608–1612, depicts the many Indian villages in the King George area at that time. Although Smith had few mapping conveniences, the outline of King George County is clear. *LOC, LC-USZ62-73508*

The *Mattacunt* and the *Ozatawomen* villages were on the south side of the Potomac River.

According to an article by George Green Shackelford, "Nanzatico, King George County, Virginia," (*Virginia Magazine of History and Biography*, October 1965) in 1676, a number of men, women, and children were killed or captured by the Susquehanna Indians only a few miles from Nanzatico. Five hundred men soon marched against the "savages," but Governor Sir William Berkeley ordered the force disbanded. This led to Bacon's Rebellion later the same year.

An article, "A River Story," written in 1986 for the *Free Lance-Star*, stated that the Nanzatico Indians living along the Rappahannock River killed John Rowley and his family. According to 1705 Richmond County court records, the murderers were hanged and a number were shipped to Antigua, where they were sold as servants. Their children under twelve were sold here and remained as servants until they reached age thirty.

As more settlers came into the area, Indians lost their land and, by 1722, many tribes were extinct.

Along both the Rappahannock and Potomac rivers, archaeologists have uncovered many small, clay pipes in which the Indians probably placed rolled-up leaves and stems. Other Indian artifacts, including shards of net-imprinted pottery, have also been discovered along with arrowpoints, hammer stones, stone mortars, pottery, stone hoes, beads, and stone axes.

— THE FIRST SETTLERS —

When the first European settlers arrived in the area known as the Northern Neck of Virginia in the first third of the seventeenth century, they found this land inhabited by Indian tribes; pristine forests; flat, cultivated land; and an abundance of game, fish, and fowl.

Many of the first European settlers migrated from the Maryland shores, where they escaped the religious intolerance imposed in the Maryland colony.

Clovis point found in King George County has been dated 10,000 to 8,000 B.C., proving that man had found his way to the western hemisphere by that time. *King George County Museum*

— The Maryland–Virginia Boundary Established —

In 1632, Charles I granted to Cecil Calvert, Baron of Baltimore, a colony north of the Potomac, including the southern bank of the river. This colony was named Maryland after the wife of Charles I, Queen Henrietta Maria. The grant specifically gave control to this colony down to the low water mark on the Potomac River. It was not until 1785 that this boundary was confirmed and the two states agreed that both states could use the river for fishing or other trade.

— Northern Neck Proprietary —

During Oliver Cromwell's reign in England, the heir to the throne, Charles II, fled with seven of his loyal followers to France. In 1649, he gave all of the land between the Rappahannock and Potomac rivers—5,282,000 acres—to those loyal seven. This area became known as the Northern Neck Proprietary. After Cromwell's death in 1658, Charles II returned to the throne and made his grant effective. Meanwhile, Thomas, Second Lord Culpeper, Baron of Thoresway, and Thomas, Fifth Baron of Cameron, had acquired the interests of the original grantees. In 1689, at the death of Lord Culpeper, his proprietary was left to his only heir, a daughter Catherine, wife of Thomas, Fifth Lord Fairfax. By law, her property became his property. Years later, the Sixth Lord of Fairfax appointed Robert Carter of Lancaster County as his agent. It is believed that William Fitzhugh, who appeared in Stafford County (now King George County) in about 1672, may have worked for the agent. Indian Town House is believed to have been a proprietary office for the agent.

Agents of the Northern Neck issued the first land grant in 1690. The grantee paid annual quitrents, or a tax, to the proprietor, releasing him from any other service. Failure to pay the quitrents or to settle the land would result in the land reverting back to the Crown. Thus the land remained under a feudal-like system until Lord Fairfax's death in 1782.

Artifacts found in the King George area, mostly on the Rappahannock River, verifying a pre-English culture. King George County Museum

— King George I —

King George County was named for King George I of England. George was born in Osnabruck, Hanover, Germany, the son of Ernest Augustus, elector of Hanover, and Sophia, granddaughter of King James I of England. George was raised in the royal court of Hanover, married Sophia, Princess of Zelle, in 1682, and had one son—the future George II—and a daughter Sophia Dorothea, who married her cousin Frederick William I, King of Prussia.

The Act of Settlement, passed by Parliament in 1700, was designed so that Sophia would become queen of England after Queen Anne's death. However, Sophia died two months before Queen Anne. Therefore, Sophia's son became King George I of England as well as ruler of Hanover.

George was a small, pale, fifty-four-year-old man when he became King of England, having lived those years in Hanover. He did not bring a queen to England from Hanover, as he had divorced his wife after her affair with a military officer. His wife was locked in a castle for the last thirty-two years of her life. Their son, the future Prince of Wales, never saw his mother during that time, which could explain the hostility that existed between him and his father through the years.

Upon his arrival in England, George faced opposition. The Jacobites, legitimate Tories, attempted to dispose of George and replace him with James Edward Stuart, the Catholic son of James II. The rebellion was a dismal failure. Because George's character and mannerisms were strictly German, and due to his ignorance of the English language and customs, he spent more than half his time in Hanover. Cabinet positions became very important in England, with the King's ministers representing the executive branch of the government and Parliament representing the legislative branch. As a result, the post of prime minister, who acted in the King's stead, was created as the majority leader in the House of Commons.

Chards of pottery found along the Rappahannock River. They depict pieces of pottery typical of American Indian origin prior to the settlement of the area by the Europeans. *King George County Museum*

George appointed only Whigs as his ministers and, together, they skillfully avoided entering European conflicts by establishing a complex web of alliances. The monarchy managed to stay out of war until George II declared war on Spain in 1739.

Although George tried dutifully to attend to his new kingdom's needs, his primary concern was always Hanover. He remained unpopular in England. After ruling England for thirteen years, George I died of a stroke on a journey to his beloved Hanover on October 11, 1727.

— FORMATION OF KING GEORGE COUNTY —

King George County was created by an act of assembly, which divided Richmond County and passed on November 24, 1720:

Left: Chestnut dugout found buried in a freshwater marsh on Machodoc Creek. It appears to have been made with European tools rather than the burning and scraping-with-clamshells method used by the American Indians. This dugout could have been made by American Indians, the English settlers, or African Americans. It is now on display at the Virginia Historical Society, Richmond. *Photo by Elizabeth Lee*

Right: William Fitzhugh (1651–1701) immigrated to Stafford County, now King George County, in about 1670. He owned about fifty-four thousand acres of land, mostly along the Potomac River. Many believe that he may have been involved as an agent for the proprietor. *Fitzhugh Family Portrait Collection, Virginia Historical Society, Richmond, Virginia*

Whereas diverse and Sundry Inconvienceys attend the Upper Inhabitants of the Said County by reason of their Great distance from the Court-House and other places usually appointed for publick meetings.

Be it therefore enacted by the Lieut. Govern. Council and Burgesses of this present General Assembly And It is hereby Enacted by the Authority thereof That from and Imediately after the Twenty Third day of Aprill which Shall be the Year of Our Lord One Thousand Seven Hundred and Twenty One The Said County of Richmond be divided into Two distinct Countys and that the Same be divided by Charles Bever dams And from the Head thereof by a North Course of Westmoreland County And that that part of the County lyeing below the Said Dams and Course remain and Shall for Ever thereafter be called and knowne by the Name of Richmond County And the Part of the County which is above the Said Dams and Course Shall be called and knowne by the Name of King George County And for the due Administration of Justice.

Be it further Enacted by the Authority aforesaid and it is hereby Enacted That after the Time aforesaid A Court for the said King George County be constantly held by the Justices thereof upon the First Friday of Every Month in Such maner as by the Laws of this Country is provided shall be by their Comission directed.

J. Randolph C H B.

This boundary extended along the Rappahannock River from Charles' Beaver Dams, or Brokenbrough Creek, westward, until in 1730 the county of Prince William was established from King George and Stafford counties, creating a western boundary of Deep Run Creek, which is now the Stafford and Fauquier County boundary line.

— Boundary Changes —

King George, as formed, did not contact the Potomac River, but was bounded on the north by Stafford County. In October 1776 (Hening's Statutes 1775–1778, p. 244, Chapter XL-1776), an act was passed "for altering and establishing the boundaries of Stafford and King George." It begins,

Whereas the present situation of the Counties of Stafford and King George is found to be very inconvenient to the inhabitants of these counties, in respect to their necessary attendance to their respective county courts and general musters, and they have petitioned that a more convenient boundary may be laid off between them: Be it therefore enacted by the General Assembly of the commonwealth of Virginia, and it is hereby enacted by the authority of the same, That from and after the first of January next the said counties of Stafford and King George shall be altered and bounded in the following manner, that is to say: Beginning at the mouth of the Muddy Creek, on the river Rappahannock, and running up the said creek, and northwest branch thereof, to a small red oak, maple and persimmon trees, at or near the head of the same branch, and between the plantations of Thomas and James Jones, thence north seventy one degrees east twenty five poles to a spring, thence down the said creek to Potowmack creek, thence down Potowmack creek to Potowmack river, and thence down the said river, pursuing the old bounds of Stafford and King George, until it strikes Rappahannock river, thence up the said river to the beginning, and those parts of the said counties of Stafford and King George, shall be the lower county, and known by the name of King George.

King George I, King of England from 1714 to 1727. *King George County Museum*

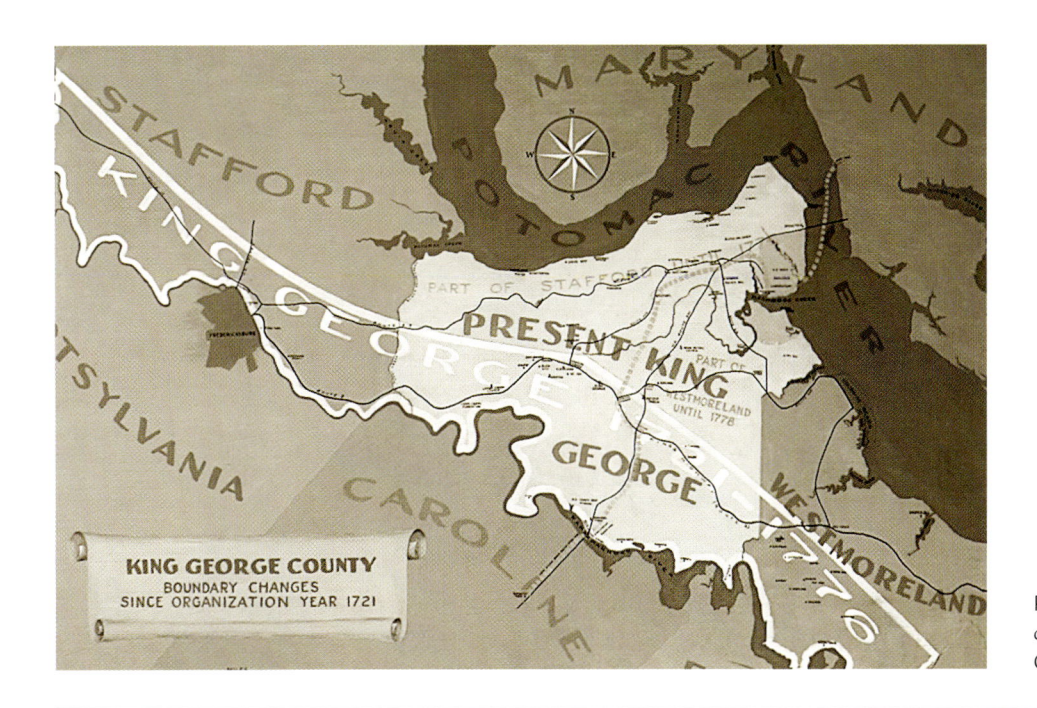

Painting, depicting county boundary changes from 1720 to 1778, by Dick Gros. *King George Courthouse*

Thus all of the land of King George on the Rappahannock River west of Muddy Creek, including the port of Falmouth, became a part of Stafford County. All that land of Stafford County on the Potomac River east of Muddy Creek became a part of King George County.

In October 1777 (Hening's Statutes 1775–1778, p. 432, Chapter XXV-1777), an act was passed to exchange land with Westmoreland County. It begins,

> *For adding part of the county of Westmoreland to the county of King George, and part of the county of King George to the county of Westmoreland, Be it enacted by the General Assembly, That from and after the twentieth day of March next all that part of the county of Westmoreland which lies above a line to be run from the head of Bristol Mine run directly to Washington's mill, on Rosier's creek, and down said creek to Potowmack river, be added to the county of King George, and that all the part of the county of King George which lies below the said line be added to the county of Westmoreland.*

Thus the King George County land east of Bristol Mine Run on the Rappahannock River became part of Westmoreland County. All of the Westmoreland County land west of Bristol Mine Run and Rosier's Creek to the Potomac River became part of King George County. The survey was done by Richmond County surveyor Griffin Garland on May 28, 1778.

These changes have remained the boundaries of the county since that time. On August 16, 2002, surveyor David Deputy re-surveyed the much-disputed boundary between King George County and Westmoreland County, placing permanent markers along the route.

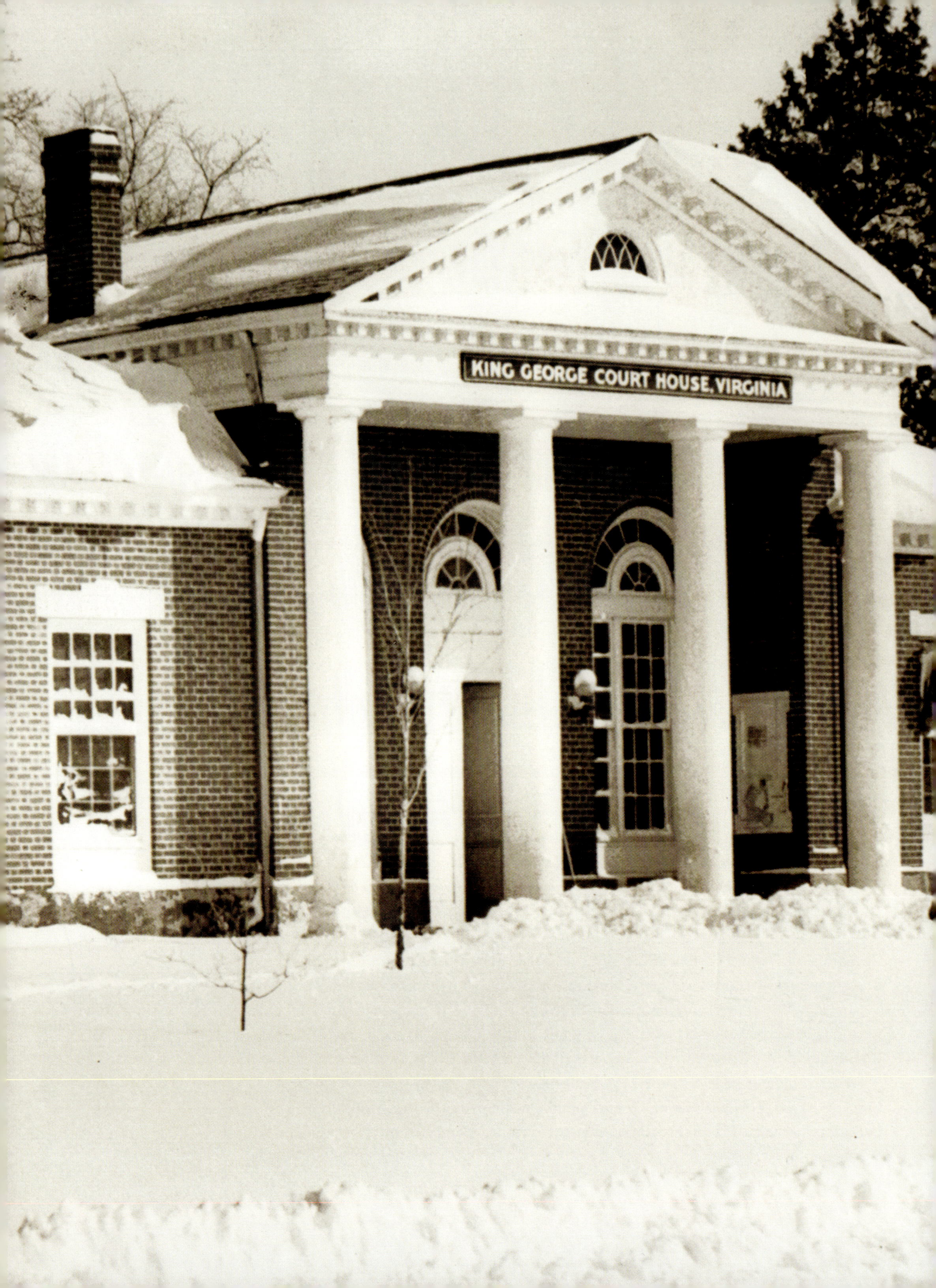
KING GEORGE COURT HOUSE, VIRGINIA

Chapter 2

County Government

— The Courthouse —

The first King George County courthouse was built on the Rappahannock River at Canning, a part of Cleve, the estate of Charles Carter. Bricks from this courthouse and the surrounding buildings can still be found at Canning, where they often surface when the ground is plowed.

The first court session was held May 19, 1721, in order to swear in the first justices. They were William Robinson, Nicholas Smith, William Thornley, Jonathan Gibson, Joseph Strother, John Spicer, and John Dinwiddie. The oath of allegiance administered to the new officials clearly demonstrates the religious connection of the Church of England with the government:

Left: Board of Supervisors, 2006, left to right: James B. Howard; Joseph W. Grzeika; C. Steven Wolfe II; Dale W. Sisson, Jr.; and Cedell Brooks, Jr. *With the permission of Joe Parker, photographer*

Right: King George County constitutional officials. Top, left to right: Treasurer Alice Campbell Moore, Clerk of Court Charles V. Mason. Bottom, left to right: Commonwealth Attorney Matthew Britton, Sheriff Clarence "Moose" Dobson, and Commissioner of Revenue Faye W. Lumpkin. *Photos by Elizabeth Lee*

I do declare that I do believe there is not any transubstantiation in the sacrament of the Lord's supper or in the elements of bread and wine at or after the consitration thereof of any person whatsoever and that the invocation or adoration of the Virgin Mary or any other saint and the sacrifice of the Mass as they are now used in the church of Rome are Superstition and Idolations.

After the justices took their oath, which was also administered to Edward Turberville, John Dinwiddie was sworn in as the first sheriff of the county, and Edward Turberville was sworn in as the first clerk of court.

After the boundary changes were made for King George County, it became evident that a more suitable location for the courthouse was needed. Land was purchased and, in about 1785, construction began on a new courthouse complex. This courthouse was the first constructed on the present site of the county courthouse. It also included a jail and a clerk's office.

The first phase of the present courthouse was constructed in 1922–1923. This consisted of the main hall, a clerk's office, and

---

Artifacts from the area where the original courthouse at Canning was located. This brick fragment is from the courthouse itself or one of the surrounding buildings there at the time court was held at Canning. *King George County Museum*

First courthouse, painted by Rufus Howland, 1976. *King George Courthouse*

King George County "Courthouse Gang," 1895. Front row seated, left to right: Col. Henry C. Purkins; Capt. Benjamin Weaver; William S. Brown, Clerk of Court; Charles H. Ashton, Circuit Court Judge; Thomas H. Bevan, Commonwealth Attorney; George W. Price, Sheriff; Joseph A. Pullen, Commissioner of Revenue; Dr. F. F. Ninde, Treasurer. Back rows, standing, left to right: Webb Miffleton or Asbury Henderson; Gusty Davis, Confederate soldier; unidentified; Willie Welch; Billy McDaniel, Magistrate Shiloh District; Hezekiah Worrell; Daniel W. Coakley, Supervisor, Potomac District; Robert Suttle, Supervisor, Shiloh District; W. W. Brown, Deputy Clerk; unidentified; Peter Wolf; T. B. Jones; William A. McKenney; John E. Mason, Circuit Court Judge, later Supreme Court Judge; Chastine Payne; Bayliss Davis; William J. Rogers, State Legislator; James Bagley King, Constable, Shiloh District; Winter Marmeduke; Sanford Morgan; Rev. John McNabb, Episcopal clergyman; unidentified; Richard Thomas Purkins; Horace Muse, Janitor; Lewis J. Billingsley; W. N. Heflin, Sheriff. *King George Courthouse*

Chapter 2: County Government

Top left: Present courthouse built in 1922–1923. Photo circa 1923. Note the horses and tractor landscaping the lawn. *Submitted by Larry and Mary Ann Cameron*

Top right: Courthouse, circa 1923. Note the Northern Neck Transportation bus in front of the courthouse on a dirt road. The Confederate monument is not on the courthouse grounds. *King George County Museum*

Bottom: First courthouse built on the present site, circa 1785. Next to it, to the right, was the clerk's office building. Photo taken in 1913. The Confederate monument is at the front of the courthouse, probably where the highway is now. It was moved when the current highway was built. *Papers of Jackson Davis, Special Collections, University of Virginia Library*

a courtroom with a balcony. The *Richmond Times-Dispatch* of May 10, 1942, described the building: "The whole effect, while undeniably compact and trim, gives a good deal the effect of an English bulldog, whose overhanging upper lip is the projecting gable of the pediment, his teeth the portico pillars, and his dewlaps the wings." A separate jail was already established on its present site. Additions were made in 1950 that gave the clerk more office space. In May 1953, an addition was added to the west side of the courthouse, adding more space for the treasurer's office. In 1949, the county joined other area counties to provide central jail services. This left the old jail vacant and available for other county services such as the Registrar's Office or the Extension Office. An assembly room was constructed in 1960 and attached to the jail building; in 1973, offices were added in the portico between the courthouse and assembly room. On April 16, 1994, a separate administration building, named the Revercomb Building in memory of Judge Horace A. Revercomb, Jr., was dedicated. Presently, plans are being considered to construct a new facility east of the present courthouse complex.

King George County has had throughout its history a series of clerks of the court that were succeeding generations of the same family. Thomas Turner was clerk of court from 1723 to 1742. His son, Harry Turner, was clerk of court from 1742 to 1752. In 1838, Solomon Brown became the clerk of court until 1845, when his son, William S. Brown, became clerk. He served until 1887 and again from 1893 to 1898, when he died while in office. William's son, William W. Brown, served as clerk of court from 1898 until 1899. Edward L. Hunter became clerk of court in 1899 and died while in office in 1909. His brother, Frederick C. S. Hunter, followed in 1909 until 1917. Lawrence B. Mason became clerk of court in 1917 and died while in office in 1960. His son, V. Elwood Mason, became clerk in 1960 and remained in office until his death in 1994. His son, C. Vic Mason, is the present clerk of court.

— County Seal —

Although not officially adopted until 1974, the King George County seal was first depicted on a float in the 1964 Fall Festival parade. Mr. Rosenberg, then

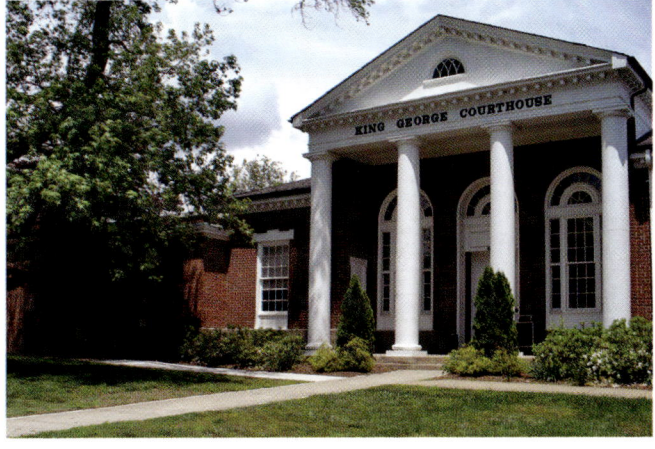

Top left: Courthouse photo, pre-1950, prior to the first additions. *Submitted by Elmer Morris, Jr.*

Top Right: King George County Courthouse. *Photo by Elizabeth Lee*

Bottom: Administration Building, dedicated in memory of "A King George County Citizen, Judge, And Man Of Community Spirit." *Photo by Elizabeth Lee*

King George County seal. *King George County Courthouse*

president of Mount Rose Canning Company, researched and compiled data for the authenticity of the design of the Royal Shield used by King George I of England. On August 8, 1974, Mr. and Mrs. Rosenberg presented the King George County Board of Supervisors with the seal depicting the county's history. "Whereas the County has been desirous of adopting a seal for official County use," the seal was approved and adopted.

The refined composition of the King George Royal Shield symbolically depicts that the foundations of America are found in the Old World. The shield is composed of four quarters. The upper left quarter is occupied by three gold lions on red that represent the Arms of England and one red lion rampant in a double tressure of fleurs-de-lis that represents the Arms of Scotland. Three fleurs-de-lis on blue occupy the upper right quarter. This area represents the Arms of France. The lower left quarter is indicated by a gold harp with silver strings and represents the Arms of Ireland as a separate kingdom. The lower right quarter of the shield consists of two gold lions on red for Brunswick II, red hearts and a blue lion rampant on gold for Luneberg III, and a white horse on red for Westphalia. In the center of the lower right quarter is Charlemagne's crown on red.

— FIRE DEPARTMENT —

On August 7, 1946, a group of men and women met at King George Courthouse to organize a fire department. The organization was called the King George Volunteer Fire Association. The first fire chief was Frank T. Hudson. Other members of the original group were Lawrence B. Mason, Jr., W. R. Garner, and W. R. Gorman.

Prior to the formation of the King George Volunteer Fire Association, firemen from Colonial Beach or Falmouth were called, or places were left to burn.

As the county grew, fire departments were established in Dahlgren and Fairview Beach. In the early 1960s, a small group of men formed the Dahlgren Volunteer Fire Group. They used a fire truck from the naval base, which was allowed to go no farther than five miles from the main gate of the base. Only an employee of the base fire department was allowed to drive the truck. Some of the members of that original group were Buster Kyle, Dick Wheat, Doug Gray, Bill Fenwick, Gilbert Moomaw, Haynes Wilkerson, Sam Robinson, Sammy Robinson, Collins Johnson, Sonny Johnson, Tommy Jewel, and Farris Portner. On October 5, 1966, the King George Volunteer Fire Association voted to send an older truck, a 1949 Chevrolet, to the Fairview Beach area. In the late 1970s, the firemen at Fairview Beach formed their own fire department.

Today, the fire departments are located on Route 3 and at Dahlgren. They are referred to as Company 1 and Company 2, respectively. Fairview Beach Fire Department, although a separate entity, is referred to as Company 3.

Photo of King George County Fire Department, circa 1951, in front of the first firehouse next to Clift Motor Company. Left to right: J. D. Hudson, Logan Clare, Elwood Mason, G. P. Gemmell, Sigsbee Clift, Gene Clift, and Jack Mason. *Submitted by Gene Clift*

HOUSE JOINT RESOLUTION NO. 395
Commending the King George Volunteer Fire Department.
Agreed to by the House of Delegates, January 10, 1997
Agreed to by the Senate, January 16, 1997
WHEREAS, in July 1946, some three dozen citizens met for the first time to discuss the creation of a volunteer fire department for King George County; and
WHEREAS, shortly thereafter, the King George Volunteer Fire Department was created, a department that has now served the citizens of King George with great distinction for 50 years; and
WHEREAS, from those humble beginnings a half-century ago, the King George Volunteer Fire Department has grown into a highly dedicated group of over 75 active firefighters who answered nearly 700 calls last year; and
WHEREAS, the King George Volunteer Fire Department now boasts two fire houses, in King George and in Dahlgren, and eight fire trucks; and
WHEREAS, in perhaps their finest hour, the King George volunteer firefighters fought a huge blaze in 1963, which consumed nearly 5,000 acres in King George and Westmoreland Counties over three days; and
WHEREAS, despite the size and duration of the conflagration, no occupied homes were lost, thanks to the extraordinary efforts of the King George volunteers; and
WHEREAS, as it celebrates its golden anniversary, the King George Volunteer Fire Department can relive with pride its 50

Chapter 2: County Government

King George County Fire Department baseball team, mid-1950s. Kneeling, left to right: Gene Clift, Chuck Leitch, Dave Blake, Charlie McGee, Bob Watts, John Motley, and Jay Newton. Standing, left to right: Sonny Ashton, A.R. Didonato, Raleigh DeShazo, Ray Kaufmann, and Max Garland. *Submitted by Gene Clift*

years of selfless, dedicated, and successful service to the citizens of King George County; now, therefore, be it
RESOLVED by the House of Delegates, the Senate concurring, That the General Assembly commend the King George Volunteer Fire Department on the occasion of its 50th anniversary; and, be it
RESOLVED FURTHER, That the Clerk of the House of Delegates prepare a copy of this resolution for presentation to Fred Clodius, president of the King George Volunteer Fire Department, as an expression of the General Assembly's congratulations and best wishes.

In 1980, as fire and rescue expanded, a new firehouse was built on Route 3 near the Route 206 intersection. Currently, this firehouse is being enlarged.

— Rescue Squad —

The Dahlgren Rescue Squad was organized in 1954 by people in the Dahlgren community who felt a need for a rescue operation in the Dahlgren and King George area. Much of the rescue work was previously performed by Colonial Beach and Fredericksburg. A converted station wagon was obtained and equipped with oxygen and first-aid supplies. Dahlgren naval base operators received emergency calls and notified duty crews.

In 1955, a small lot of land was donated on Route 206, and a building was constructed by members of the squad and friends who donated their time.

In 1978, the Biomedical Telemetry System began operation as the first link in the emergency communications chain, bringing doctors to the patients before their arrival at the hospital.

In 1979, Station Two was completed on Route 3 near the Route 206 intersection, next to the firehouse. The Dahlgren station was referred to as Station One.

— TELEPHONE SERVICE —

The first telephone in King George County was believed to be at the King George Motor Company. The date is unknown. By 1942, there were forty-three telephones in King George, their listings filling one page of an area phone pamphlet. Numbers were four digits. Among the telephone users were Thomas E. Lee of Shiloh, Webster Allensworth of Rollins Fork, Friendly Cottage in Goby, and Mrs. Peyton Parker at Index.

Until 1954, telephone service between King George and Dahlgren was a toll call. Tidewater Telephone Company began the changeover in September 1953. At the same time, the county shifted to a more standard dialing convention of five digits, so that "no two telephones in the state will have the same number."

The prefixes for King George County, 775 and 663, were once SPruce 5 and NOrth 3.

— LEWIS EGERTON SMOOT LIBRARY —

Ann Hopewell Smoot built Lewis Egerton Smoot Library in 1969 in memory of her husband. The library was designed after the Mentor Public Library in Mentor, Ohio. Mrs. Smoot operated and privately funded the library from March 1970 until November 1973. The Board of Supervisors adopted an ordinance on October 18, 1973, to create a board of trustees. On November 1, 1973, Mrs. Smoot donated the land, the library building, and its contents to King George County. She also donated $700,000 to establish an endowment fund to maintain the library.

Top: Dahlgren Rescue Squad garage, circa 1965. *Submitted by Betty Lou Braden*
Bottom: Lewis Egerton Smoot Library. *Submitted by Betty Lou Braden*

Chapter 2: County Government

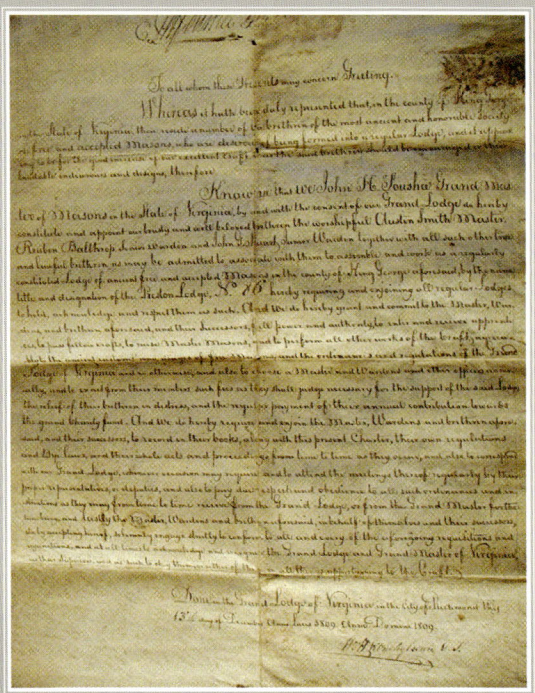

Top: Barnesfield Park. *Photo by Jean Graham*

Middle left: Wayside Park on the Potomac. *Photo by Jean Graham*

Middle right: In 2005, the Hudson-Morris Lodge received the original Charter of Preston Lodge No. 86. *Photo by Elizabeth Lee*

Bottom: Community service sign, constructed by Will Taylor for his Eagle Scout badge. *Photo by Jean Graham*

30 *King George County: A Pictorial History*

— BARNESFIELD PARK —

Barnesfield Park was once part of Barnesfield plantation, the home of the Hooe family since the early 1700s. Barnesfield Park was deeded to the county in 1972 by the U.S. government, which had increased its holdings to include the Barnesfield tract earlier in its development of the naval base. However, the base never expanded. The tract contained 157 acres of land. The Board of Supervisors designated the area as a public park. Today, the park boasts baseball fields, playgrounds, trails, and picnic areas.

— WAYSIDE PARK —

The three-acre Wayside Park, also a part of Barnesfield, has been a favorite for King George County residents for generations. It has been used for fishing, swimming, and picnicking, as well as a public landing.

Mount Bethel Retreat Center. *Mount Bethel Association*

— COMMUNITY ORGANIZATIONS —

King George County has a variety of organizations beneficial to the county. Organizations range from community service groups to fraternal orders. Many, such as the Ratcliffe, Owens, Sumner Post No. 89, American Legion, have their own meeting facilities.

On December 13, 1809, a charter was issued authorizing Preston Lodge No. 86 to be established to operate as a legally constituted Masonic Lodge of Ancient Free and Accepted Masons. The lodge met at the King George Courthouse area until 1818, when it was declared dormant. Not until 1848 was the lodge revived. The Hudson-Morris Lodge No. 80 was chartered February 11, 1981.

The first meeting of the King George Lodge No. 314 Free and Accepted Masons, Prince Hall Affiliated, was held at Ralph Bunche High School Auditorium on September 21, 1951. A charter was issued on December 30, 1951. After the initial meeting, the lodge met in the Odd Fellows Hall from October 10, 1951, to October 9, 1963, when the lodge purchased the building from the Odd Fellows. A new lodge was built and opened on September 2, 1978.

The Mount Bethel Baptist Association was organized in 1875 at Mt. Zion Baptist Church in Arlington, Virginia. In 1901, members of churches of the District of Columbia, Maryland, and Virginia purchased a parcel of land in King George County to be known as the "Old Folks Home." A pavilion, playground, kiddie boats and kiddie trains, a beach house, and toilets were added in 1970. In the early 1980s, renovation was done on the pavilion and the mansion. Mount Bethel is now a retreat center overlooking the Potomac River.

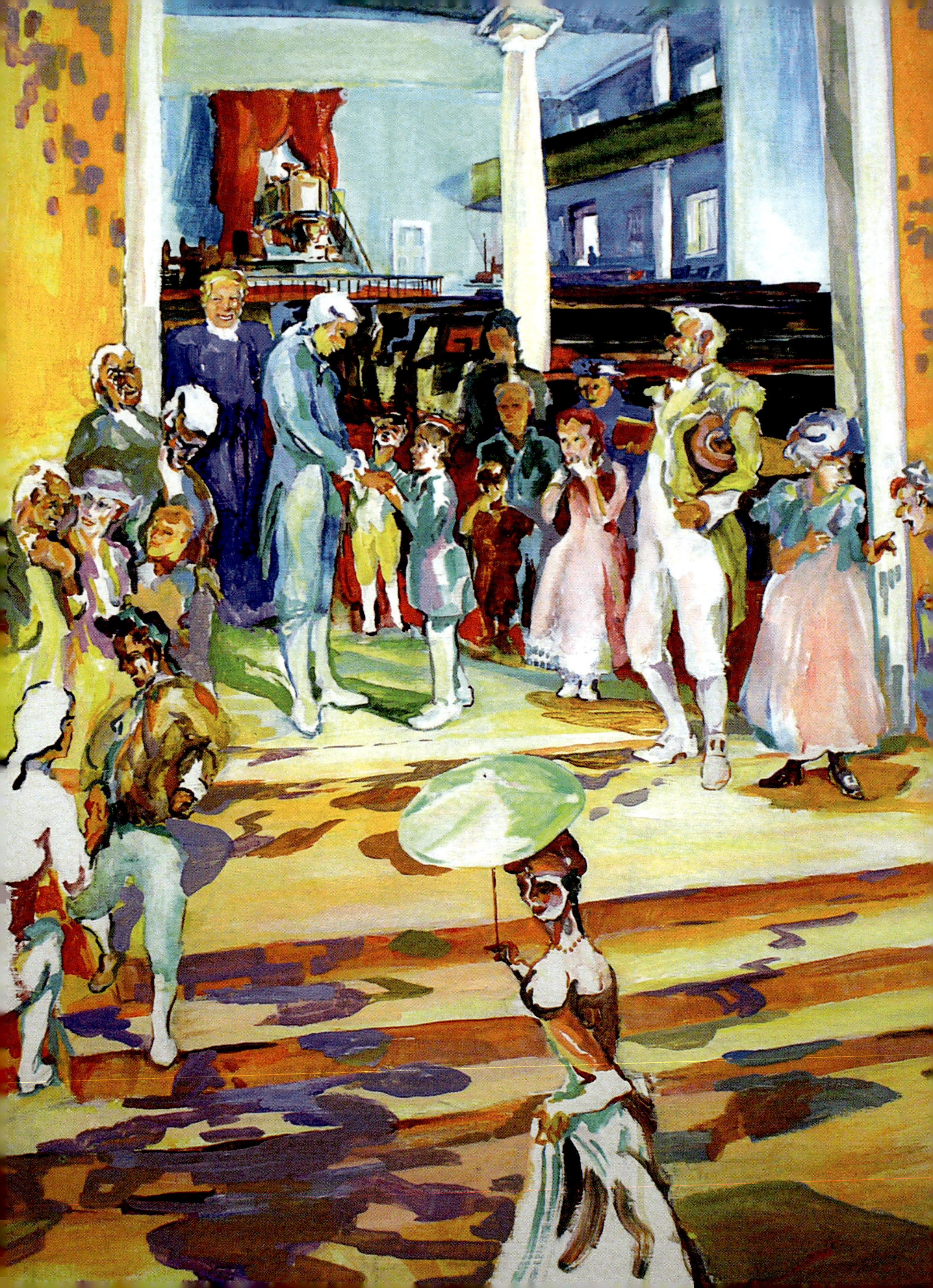

Chapter 3
People Who Left Their Mark

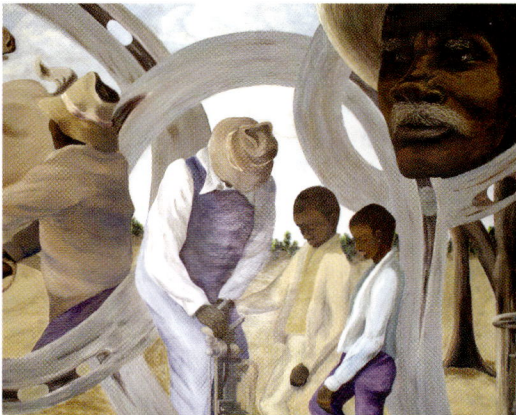

From the famous to the not-so-famous, every person who has ever lived in King George County has left a lasting mark on our history. From the great teachers who made a profound difference, to the man down the road who made us feel a part of something bigger, King George County has its standout figures. We can only present a few.

— George Washington —

Although the plantation today lies in Stafford County, Augustine Washington moved his family in about 1735 to King George County to the Strother plantation, where he died in 1743. Today, it is referred to as Ferry Farm. Augustine Washington's will was recorded in King George County. George

Washington, the first president of the United States, lived all of his young life—from the time he was three years old until he left his mother's home—in King George County. In addition to visiting his brother at Mount Vernon, George also visited family in the Chotank area of King George County, then Stafford County, where he frequently visited his cousins, dined at Hylton, and attended St. Paul's Church.

— JAMES MADISON —

In the 1750s, on the northern Rappahannock River shore across from Port Royal, Rebecca Moore lived quietly. Rebecca had been married to a wealthy, influential merchant, Francis Conway, in the Port Royal area. Francis and Rebecca were the parents of seven children, the youngest being Eleanor Rose Conway. The young widow Rebecca had remarried John Moore, another merchant of the area. In September 1749, her youngest daughter married James Madison, a young merchant, and moved with him to the wilderness area of present Orange County. Eleanor returned to her mother's home, where she gave birth to her first child, James Madison, on March 16, 1751. He was baptized at the Strother Church, believed to be located northeast of the home, and soon was taken back to the wilderness where he grew up. It is unlikely that he spent any time in King George with his grandmother because Rebecca died in 1760. Today, no one knows exactly where her house was located. Many believe that it is the large plantation house called Belle Grove, but that house was not built until 1851. Many others believe that it is perhaps a smaller portion or room of that same plantation house. However, elderly gentlemen of King George County deposed in 1892 that, as children, they had played on the ruins of the old house said to be the birthplace of the fourth president of the United States. All of their depositions stated that the house stood east of the large house, between the house and the yard fence.

James Madison, known as the Father of the Constitution, was a representative to the Virginia Convention in 1776 and led a successful fight for the Statute for Religious Freedom. He was the youngest delegate to the Continental Congress

Top: This painting, which hangs in the courthouse, depicts the frequent visits George Washington made to St. Paul's Church. Painted by Jack Darling in 1976. *King George County Courthouse*

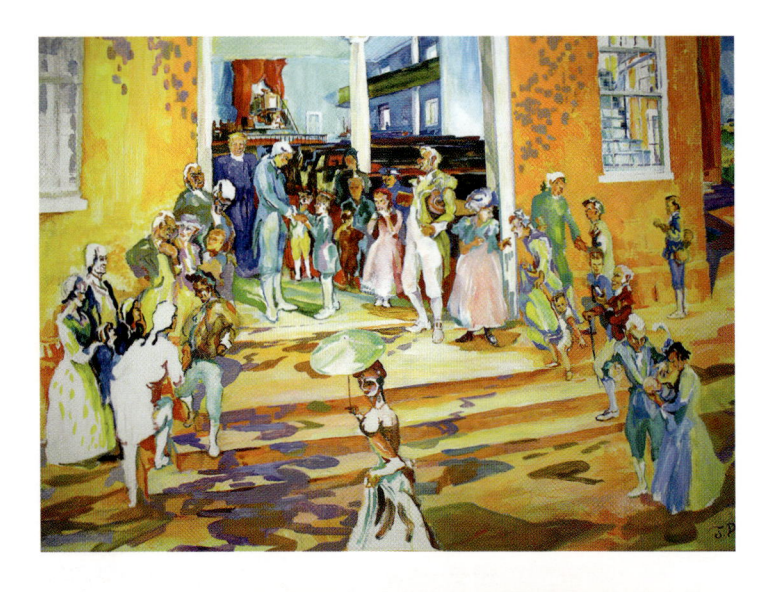

Bottom: Last will and testament of Augustine Washington. *King George County Courthouse Record*

Left: James Madison, fourth president of the United States, was born in King George County. *LOC, LC-USZ62-87924*
Right: This painting of James Madison hangs in the courthouse. Artist is unknown. *King George County Courthouse*

in 1781. In 1787, while the details of our government system were being forged, Madison wrote the Virginia Plan, which suggested that representation in the legislature be proportionate to population of the state. The opposition proposed a one-state, one-vote plan. A compromise was reached, and the two-chamber system of legislature was established—one proportionate to population and one by state. In 1788, Madison was elected to the House of Representatives. He was a chief organizer of the Democratic-Republican party, opposing the Federalist party. He became secretary of state under the Jefferson administration. In 1809, James Madison became the fourth president of the United States. During his term, which lasted until 1817, the United States again fought with Great Britain in the War of 1812.

Besides his uncompromising stand on religious freedom, James Madison pleaded with the new nation for "eventual extinguishment of slavery in the United States." Madison died in June 1836.

— Joseph Jones —

Joseph Jones was born in 1727 in King George County to James and Hester Davis Jones. James emigrated from Wales in the early 1700s, settled in King George County, and in 1726 married the widow Hester Davis Lampton. He and Hester had three daughters, Hester, Elizabeth, and Blanche, and one son, Joseph. He acquired a sizable amount of land for himself and family and was financially able to send young Joseph to London for schooling. James died in the spring of 1744. Most of the estate was left to young Joseph.

Chapter 3: People Who Left Their Mark

Joseph studied law at the Inns of Court in London and was made a member of the English bar in 1751. He returned to King George in 1752 and two years later was appointed the King's attorney for King George County. Additionally, he had opened a law office in Fredericksburg.

In 1771, he was elected a member of his church vestry in King George. This was considered the first step to elected office. In 1772, Joseph decided to run for a seat in the House of Burgesses. He won and took his seat with his fellow King George burgess, William Fitzhugh of Chatham. When Lord Dunmore dissolved the assembly and called for new elections in 1775, Jones repeated his victory.

He married Mary Taliaferro, the daughter of Colonel John Taliaferro of Spotsylvania's Snow Creek plantation.

When Spence Monroe died in 1774, James Monroe began an association with his uncle, Joseph Jones, that would last until death separated them. Jones continued paying James's tuition at William & Mary and advised him. In 1774, in King George County, Joseph Jones was elected chairman of the Committee of Safety. Others on the committee were John Taliaferro, John Skinker, Francis Conway, John Pollard, and William Fitzhugh.

During the 250th anniversary of the birth of James Madison, King George County Historical Society members visit with their "cousins" in 2001. *Submitted by Elizabeth Lee*

When Dunmore dissolved the assembly, the burgesses continued to meet at the Raleigh tavern in Williamsburg. This became the First Virginia Convention. Jones was there representing his county. These men adopted the Fairfax Resolves forbidding the importation of slaves or goods into Virginia after November 1, 1774, and all exports to Great Britain after August 1775. They also chose delegates to the First Continental Congress.

In 1775, Jones returned to the House of Burgesses and was installed as chair of the Committee of Courts and Justice. The assembly was divided on the issue of peaceful resolution or independence and war. The second convention met in March 1775 in Richmond at St. John's Church. Here, Jones and his fellow delegates chose representatives to the Second Continental Congress and authorized the arming of the militia for the defense of the colony.

The Third Virginia Convention was called in July–August 1775. They chose a colony-wide Committee of Safety as an executive council to act when the conventions were not in session. Jones was appointed to this elite body. The convention also ordered the recruitment of two regiments of regular soldiers and sixteen battalions of minutemen.

In December of that year, the Fourth Convention met, again with Jones as a delegate. They created a Virginia navy, continued the Committee of Safety for another year, created a Court of Admiralty to enforce trade restrictions, and established county commissions to try loyalists who bore arms against the colonies. His Committee of Safety had to choose a military leader to lead troops against the former Governor Dunmore. They selected William Woodford, of Caroline County and Fredericksburg, to lead the expedition. Woodford, with six years experience in the French and Indian War, defeated Dunmore in the Battle of Great Bridge.

In 1776, in Virginia, the fifth and last Virginia Convention met in Williamsburg in May 1776, to create a new state of Virginia. One of their primary actions was the passing of a resolution calling for independence. Thomas Jefferson wrote the resolution, based on thoughts from his fellow Virginians, including Joseph Jones. This was sent to their delegates in Philadelphia, and Richard Henry Lee introduced it in the Continental Congress. As a result, the committee to draft a declaration to the King was created.

But the Virginia Convention was seeking to draft a declaration of rights and a state constitution. Joseph Jones was appointed to the committee. While it is true that we owe much to George Mason for its writing, all members had their say in its creation, including Joseph Jones.

> *That all men are by nature equally free and independent, and have certain inherent rights, of which, when they enter into a state of society, they cannot, by any compact, deprive or divest their prosperity; namely, the enjoyment of life and liberty, with the means of acquiring and possessing property, and pursuing and obtaining happiness and safety.*
> —Virginia Declaration of Rights, Section 1, 1776

In 1776, Joseph Jones was elected to the newly adopted House of Delegates. In 1777, he was chosen to represent Virginia in the Continental Congress.

Jones's wife died in 1777. Late in 1777, he was reelected by the Virginia Assembly to serve a second term as congressman but he declined.

In 1778, Jones accepted an appointment to the Virginia General Court as a justice. In later years, this became the Supreme Court, the highest court in the land. About 1779, he remarried to the widow Mary Waugh Dawson of Orange County. A son, Joseph, Jr., was born in 1779.

In 1779, Jones represented Virginia in Congress and temporarily gave up his seat on the General Court. He served in Congress for the next three years. Jones spent many hours in deliberations and discussions with the Virginia Assembly on behalf of the new country to convince Virginia to turn over the northwestern territory to the new country to develop into western states and to have bounty land. He eventually won their approval to cede the land to the new national government.

With his backing, James Monroe was elected to Jones's vacated seat in the assembly representing King George County in 1782.

Jones left Congress in 1783 and was replaced by his nephew, James Monroe. Jones returned to Virginia as a delegate from King George County in the General Assembly (1784–1785). He was appointed to the Virginia Council of State from 1785–1789. He then returned to his seat on the General Court, a seat he held until his death.

Jones built a fine house in Fredericksburg. He also resided at Spring Hill in King George. His second wife died in 1787.

The following year, Virginia debated whether it would ratify the new U.S. Constitution. Eight states had ratified it, and many others looked toward Virginia to guide them in their deliberations. Virginia was torn. Although Jones lost his bid to attend, he was considered by many to be a tremendous influence on the actions taken by the attendees in the ratification process. He corresponded extensively with James Madison recommending changes. The Constitution was approved with a Bill of Rights.

Judge Jones died on October 26, 1805, while in Fredericksburg. Ideologically, he lived on in James Monroe. Monroe's biographer, Harry Ammon, says this about Jones: "Highly esteemed by his contemporaries, he enjoyed the confidence of Washington, Jefferson and Madison, who prized him for the soundness of his counsel." He further adds, "Monroe as an adult, resembled his uncle in many ways—reflective, never rushing to conclusions but forming opinions deliberately. The same tact, warmth and patience in human relations, so pronounced in the Judge's character, were equally apparent in the nephew."

In Monroe's autobiography, he states about his uncle, "Few men possessed in a higher degree the confidence and esteem of his fellow citizens, or merited it more, for soundness of intellect, perfect integrity, and devotion to his country."

William "Extra Billy" Smith. *Drawing by Jean Moore Graham*

— WILLIAM "EXTRA BILLY" SMITH —

Another influential merchant/farmer of the eighteenth century in King George was Thomas Smith. The father of eight children, he owned property in several areas of the county. Caleb, one of his younger sons, married Mary Waugh, and in 1802 bought a plantation called Marengo on Rosier's Creek. William Smith was born on September 6, 1797. Historians debate his birthplace. William Smith claimed that he was born at Marengo. But Marengo was not purchased by his father until 1802. Others believe that he was born at Office Hall, the home of his paternal grandfather. William was schooled in King George, but moved by the time he was eighteen years old to Fauquier County, after the death of his father, to pursue his law training. As a young man, he established a mail service. During this time, he obtained the nickname "Extra Billy" as a sarcastic remark from a senator that targeted Smith and his unofficial mail route in tirades on the Senate floor. In 1836, William Smith was elected state senator and became a vocal critic of state banks and a champion of internal improvements. He was elected to the House of Representatives in 1841 and, in January 1846, was appointed governor of Virginia. While governor, he asked the General Assembly to provide for Virginia counties who wanted to have free schools. The system went into effect in October 1847. After participating in the gold rush, Smith returned to Congress in 1853, until he enlisted in the Forty-ninth Virginia Regiment. In November 1861, he was elected to the Confederate Congress, but never left his regiment. On December 31, 1863, he resigned his commission as major general, and, on January 1, 1864, he was sworn in as the governor of Virginia. His main objectives for this term were building a strong home defense and attempting to meet the needs of the Confederate soldiers. On April 2, 1865, Smith ordered the evacuation of the state government, all state papers, and state funds to Lynchburg. Following the war, he was initially prohibited to seek office. Smith returned to his home in Warrenton, but in 1875, he was elected to the Virginia House of Delegates representing Fauquier County until 1879. William Smith died at his Warrenton home on May 18, 1887.

— Thomas Lomax Hunter —

Thomas Lomax Hunter was born in King George on March 6, 1875, to Frederick Campbell Stuart Hunter and his wife, Susan Rose Turner, of Belle Grove. Frederick was clerk of the court for King George County from 1909 to 1917. Thomas was a writer and, in 1895, the local paper reported that he was off to Richmond to write. In 1918 and 1920, Hunter was elected to represent King George and Stafford counties in the Virginia House of Delegates. During World War I, he served as the food administrator for King George County. Hunter's writings were successful and, from 1929 until his death, he wrote a column in the *Richmond Times-Dispatch* called "As It Appears to the Cavalier." Hunter was also a poet and, in 1948, the General

This painting of Thomas Lomax Hunter at Waverley was painted by D. McCleskey in 1976. *King George County Courthouse*

Assembly named him poet laureate of Virginia. Thomas married Marie Doherty, whose maternal grandfather was William S. Brown, clerk of the court during the Civil War. He and his wife made their home at Waverley, which had belonged to William S. Brown. Thomas Lomax Hunter died on June 19, 1948.

— THOMAS BENTON GAYLE —

Thomas Benton Gayle III was born at Altoona Farm, west of Fredericksburg, to Thomas Benton Gayle, Jr., and his wife, Ellen Jane Pratt, on December 20, 1899. In 1910, after the death of his grandfather, Alexander Pratt, he and his family moved to Aspen Grove Farm in King George County. He attended schools in Stafford County and Fredericksburg. He spent a short period of time in the Army Transportation Service during World War I. After the war, he attended Virginia Polytechnic Institute where he majored in agricultural education. Upon graduation in June 1923, he accepted a position as agricultural instructor in Westmoreland County. On July 1, 1925, T. Benton Gayle became the superintendent of schools in the newly formed division of schools for King George and Stafford counties. At the time, he was the youngest superintendent in the State of Virginia. Mr. Gayle remained in this position until 1965, when he retired. Of the King George County School Board, T. Benton Gayle stated, "The people of King George County were just about the best people that a man could work with…people like Dr. Minor, Thomas Lomax Hunter, Wayland Coakley, Emerson Purks, Wayland Clarke, Junior Morris, Stuart Ashton, and others who were excellent members of the school board." Mr. Gayle died in 1989.

— CAROLINUS PEYTON —

By far, one of the most colorful characters of King George County history is Carolinus Peyton. His portrait may be seen in the gallery surrounding the halls of King George Courthouse. Carolinus represents the lost art of blacksmithing that was once so much a vital part of our county history. In the days before the automobile, a blacksmith or the wheelwright was the mechanic that saw to it that our transportation needs were met. Even after the advent of the automobile, many King George County residents depended on the keepers of the old trade well into the twentieth century. Horses still needed shoes; wagons still needed repair. In October 1976, *National Geographic* published "A Long Life, a Good Life on the Potomac," featuring Carolinus and his trade.

Carolinus was born April 25, 1887, in Tetotum, King George County, to Wesley Peyton and his wife, Lydia Lucas. His father was a slave at Spy Hill, also in Tetotum. His mother was probably also born a slave. According to Carolinus,

Top: T. Benton Gayle, superintendent of King George Schools, 1925-1965. *King George County Museum*

Bottom: Carolinus Peyton (1887-1986). *King George County Museum*

Left: The life of Carolinus Peyton is depicted in this 1976 painting. The artist is unknown. *King George Courthouse*
Right: James Monroe, fifth president of the United States, owned land in King George County. *LOC, LC-USZ62-104958*

he was hired out to Silas Redman to help his wife at their store on Rosier Creek. During this time, at the age of ten, while carrying water to a ship docked nearby, Carolinus was kidnapped and taken to the Eastern Shore for several years, working under "near-slavery" conditions. According to Carolinus, he went to New Jersey for many years, and then traveled to Sweden with a young man who helped him learn the trade of blacksmithing and wheelwrighting. Carolinus stated that he also traveled through Europe, Asia, and Africa before returning to King George. By this time, most of his family was gone, and no one knew him. Carolinus learned the art of breaking mules, preferring them to horses. He bought a small piece of property near his birthplace, married, and lived there until his death on February 24, 1986. He was buried at Good Hope Baptist Church, where he had been an active member and deacon.

— James Monroe —

James Monroe, fifth president of the United States, was the son of Spence Monroe and his wife, Elizabeth Jones. Elizabeth was the sister of Joseph Jones. Her marriage to Spence Monroe is referenced in King George County Deed Book 4, when her father gave property to her. In 1783, James Monroe represented King George County in the General Assembly. In June 1788, a deed was recorded in King George County transferring three hundred acres of land owned by James Monroe of Fredericksburg and William Bankhead to James Monroe of Westmoreland County. The land was described as "Glebe Hanover" and previously being in Washington Parish in Westmoreland County.

Above: Sam Dishman (sheriff, 1943–1959) and Cleveland Grigsby (treasurer, 1923–1967). Photo circa 1958. *Submitted by James Dallas Dishman*

Above: Jay Powell, sheriff of King George County, 1959–1975. *Submitted by Barbara Powell*

Above: Dr. Roger Harris was a county icon until the 1980s. He made housecalls to King George from his home in Port Royal at all hours to deliver babies or treat feverish children. *Submitted by Elmer Morris, Jr.*

Above left: Joseph Johnson (1879–1968), a Spanish-American War veteran, with one of his grandsons. Mr. Johnson was the first African American sheriff's deputy in King George County. *Submitted by Phyllis Ashton*

Above right: Raymond Rock lived in King George from 1941 until his death in 1993. He worked as a fireman at the Naval Proving Grounds, and later as a mechanic at Port Royal Motor Company. In 1951, he began operating a service station near the courthouse. He left in 1979, when the highway was widened and cut off the front of his business. He never knew a stranger. He was often seen in his tow truck helping stranded motorists. In 1978, he received an Outstanding Citizen Award from the Veterans of Foreign Wars for "fine reputation built on fairness, honesty and compassion for those In need." *Photograph by Elizabeth Lee*

John Wilkes Booth.
LOC, LC-USZ62-25166

— JOHN WILKES BOOTH: A VISITOR OF NOTE —

In April 1865, General Lee had surrendered to General Grant at Appomattox. King George County was still occupied by federal troops. John Wilkes Booth, in a last ditch effort to turn the tide, shot President Abraham Lincoln at Ford's Theater in Washington, D.C., on April 14, 1865. He made his escape through Maryland, stopping at the home of Dr. Mudd to have his ankle repaired, and then to the Potomac River.

Crossing the heavily guarded river at night, Booth made his way up Gambo's Creek to the home of Mrs. Rose Quesenberry, a widow with small children. There, Booth received care before he continued his escape. Later, Mrs. Quesenberry was arrested and taken to Washington for aiding in Booth's escape. In a note to the county clerk, she summarized her thoughts, "People will think what they want."

Booth continued on to Cleydael, the summer home of Dr. Richard Stuart. For reasons unknown, Dr. Stuart was suspicious of his unexpected visitors and asked Booth and his traveling companions to leave. Later, Dr. Stuart was exonerated of any charges because of the note Booth left, criticizing his hospitality. Booth spent the night near Cleydael, and the next morning a neighbor carried Booth by wagon to the Rappahannock River.

At Port Conway, he met William Rollins, who agreed to ferry him across the river at a later time. Once across the river, William Rollins told the federal troops about his passenger. This eventually led to the confrontation and death of John Wilkes Booth at Garrett's Farm, south of Port Royal.

Chapter 3: People Who Left Their Mark

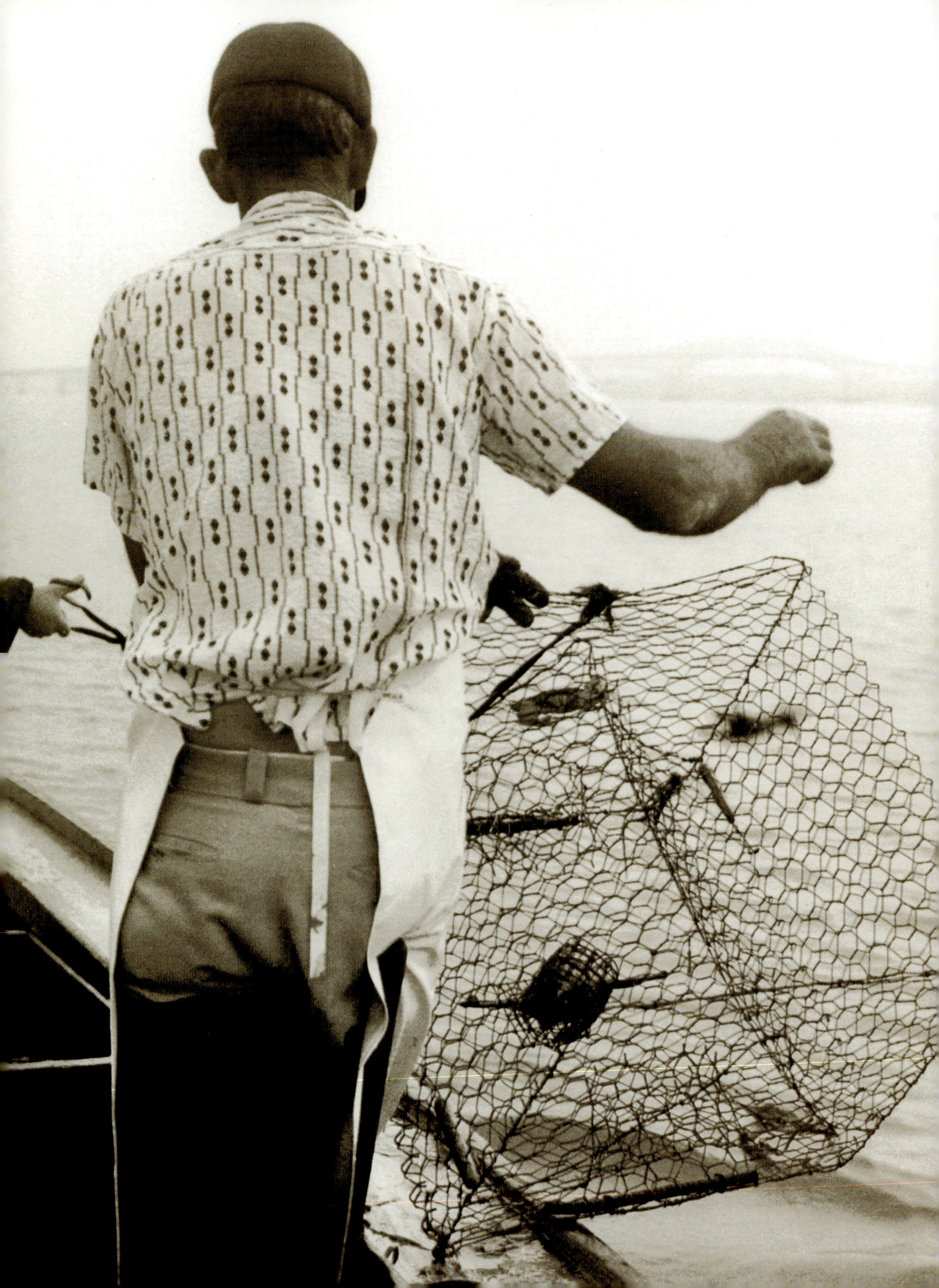

Chapter 4
Making a Living

"As a work of art, I know few things more pleasing to the eye, or more capable of affording scope and gratification to a taste for the beautiful, than a well-situated, well-cultivated farm."

—Edward Everett,
October 9, 1857

From its earliest history, King George County was a rural area of large plantation owners, small farmers, and fishermen. Farmers raised sheep, hogs, and cattle. Farmland produced corn, wheat, and barley. The earliest crops included tobacco and some cotton.

Farms always had access to the river for transporting goods. Slave labor worked fields prior to the War Between the States and emancipation.

Top left: Wheat being harvested at Spy Hill. *Submitted by Ruth Taliaferro*
Top right: County Agent George Hall working at "the grass roots" with a King George County farmer, circa 1955. *King George County Museum*
Bottom left: Three generations of farmers in King George County: Billie H. Weedon; his son, Billie T. Weedon; and grandson, Tommy Weedon. Photo taken in 1984, Chestnut Hill. *Submitted by Gloria Sharp*
Bottom right: Baled hay in the Sealston area. *King George County Museum*

    Thus large plantations flourished. Prior to the war, large estates were rarely divided. Following the war, such large plantations could not be supported, due to lack of available labor. It was considered best to divide the estate. Thus many of the old, large plantations were sold off into small farms.

    The number of farms and farm acreage is rapidly declining. In 2002, there were only 169 working farms in King George County, containing 31,888 acres, of which 11,746 acres were harvested farmland. In 2005, there were only 2,700 cattle and cows in the county.

    Fishing on both the Potomac and Rappahannock rivers has been a large business in King George. In April 1896, an unknown reporter from Comorn wrote in his column for the *Richmond Times*:

White-faced herd on good pasture. *King George County Museum*

Sheep at Panorama. Photo by Ralph E. Fall, 1971. *Virginia Department of Historic Resources, Richmond, Virginia*

Left: Farmer John King learned to drive his father's tractor at an early age. *Submitted by Bobbe King*

Right: Today, fields of spinach grow on Oaken Brow Farm. *Photo by Elizabeth Lee*

It is said that some of the herrings caught on the Potomac this week are the largest ever taken from that river. Some of the fishermen, who were discouraged some weeks ago because of continued unfavorable weather in the early and middle part of the season, are now in high spirits, and are working with renewed hopes and great zeal since fish became so plentiful last week. One of the Potomac seines caught 60,000 herrings at one haul the other day, besides a correspondingly large quantity of shad, perch, cat, rock, and other marketing fish. But the season being so far advanced, and the finny-tribe so uncertain in their movements, the fishermen would not be surprised for any change of this to bring a change in their "luck."

— Bristol Iron Works —

In 1724, the Bristol Iron Works was established for the John King Company of Bristol, England. Augustine Washington, the father of George Washington, and John Tayloe of Mount Airy both had an interest in iron works. Low-grade iron ore was smelted into pig iron, shipped to England, and made into iron goods. These goods were shipped back and sold in the Virginia colony. By 1730, the

Bristol Iron Works was abandoned. Evidence points to a possibility that there was also a glass works on the same site.

— ROBERT WALKER —

King George County was not without its artisans. Robert Walker, born in Scotland, later living in King George in the early to mid-1700s, crafted furniture for such families as the Carters, Fitzhughs, Lees, and Washingtons.

Thomas Purkins handcrafted canes or walking sticks. Several of them have survived.

— CANNERIES —

In support of the small farms of the county, several canneries came into existence. In 1929, the King George Cannery was organized. It was located at Greenlaw's Wharf on the Rappahannock River. A cannery also was set up at

Left: Ernest Green prepares his crab nets for a day on the river. *Submitted by Alma Gaddis*
Top right: This label was from a product canned at the King George Farmers Cooperative, Inc., cannery. Date is unknown. *King George Museum*
Bottom right: Typical iron furnace such as the one at Bristol Mines. *Drawing by Jean Graham*

Chapter 4: Making a Living

Old Washington Mill, the longest-operating mill in the county, painted by Jack Darling, 1976. *King George Courthouse*

Berry's Wharf. A community cannery was located behind the courthouse in King George. Housewives took their produce to the canneries and processed them there.

— MILLS —

Another vital support for the local farmers was the gristmill. Farmers brought their corn or wheat for grinding. Several such mills were in existence in King George County since its earliest history.

Garnett's Mill, on Rosier's Creek, was once known as Baber's Mill and Washington's Mill. Immigrant John Washington built it in about 1665. In 1675, he gave this mill to his son, Lawrence Washington (George Washington's grandfather), who in turn willed it to his son John. It remained in the Washington family until 1808, when Thomas Turner bought it.

Washington's Mill on the Machodoc Creek at Windsor Plantation remained in operation until 1942, when floodwaters ended its usage. Reconstructed in about 1805, the mill probably dates back to the early 1700s. Since Windsor was not owned by the Washingtons until about 1830, the mill was probably a Thornton mill and later named for Henry Thacker Washington, a cousin of George Washington.

Mason's Mill at Alto was mentioned several times in an 1878–1880 Caledon farm journal. Kings Mill on Kings Mill Creek and Fitzhugh's Mill on Lamb's Creek are only a few of the dozens of mills once scattered throughout the county.

— Vulcan Brick Company —

In March of 1897, Wilmont Fire Proofing Company of West Virginia leased four hundred acres from Sarah Montgomery of Toby's Point. The purpose of the lease was to mine and mill the minerals and metals, which were used to manufacture solid bodies for fire-proofing fire brick, pipe and boiler covers, filters, tiles, and other brick products. Such material could be manufactured from diatomaceous earth found in the high cliffs at Toby's Point and was ideal for stronger and more porous brick for furnace construction.

Clay was dug from the bank and a level place was made for the kilns, dryers, sheds, and track for tramcars to transport the brick and clay. A wharf was built for the barges that were used to transport the brick to Baltimore, Washington, Norfolk, and Providence, Rhode Island. People and goods also came into this landing. A hotel was constructed for the travelers and laborers. In May 1909, Vulcan Brick Company bought out Wilmont. Vulcan, in addition to making brick, sold the diatoms to be used for the manufacturing of soap, paints, pottery, and dynamite.

Left: Remains of Kings Mill on Kings Mill Creek in King George County. *Virginia Department of Historic Resources, Richmond, Virginia*
Right: Mill stone, now used as a step, found on Mount Pleasant property and believed to be from a mill on the farm. *Submitted by Elizabeth Lee*

In 1929, the American Diatom Corporation of Philadelphia bought the interest in the mining operation. This company remained until 1934, when the entire operation was abandoned.

Today, the 365 acres of Toby's Point include only a dock and parking area, and the remainder is part of the Rappahannock River Valley National Wildlife Refuge. Signs of the brick manufacturing can still be seen in pieces of the brick labeled "Wilmont" or "Vulcan," in the remains of the foundation of the manager's house, or in the pieces of a partially submerged barge.

— The Local Store —

Areas within walking distance were supported by a local grocery store and post office. It was common for stores to be within a mile or two of each other. Goods were shipped by boat and transported by wagon by the storeowner to his store. Goods were also bought from the local farmers.

— Hotels and Motels —

Within the area of the courthouse, there would have been an inn, usually located within a tavern, where those traveling distances to the courthouse could stay. An 1805 plat of the courthouse area shows such a tavern in the area that is now known as "the old hotel."

With the construction of Highway 301 through King George in 1940, several motels opened to the new traveling generation. They remained in operation until the 1960s, when the new north–south Interstate 95 was constructed to the west of King George.

— Dairies —

Dairies have been in existence over the history of our county. One of the oldest was Barnesfield Dairy at the sight of the plate battery on the naval base, near the Potomac River. Operating in the 1920s, it closed around 1939 when the government took over the property to expand the Naval Proving Grounds. A more recent dairy was Hopyard Farm Dairy, which was in existence into the 1960s.

Top: Brick furnace at Wilmont. *Submitted by Sue Williams*
Bottom: Brick made at Wilmont. *King George Museum*

Above and left: Thornton McDaniel opened his store in the mid-1930s, less than a mile from his father's store at Gera. Photo taken about 1939. Insert picture of the store was taken after it had closed. *Submitted by Ruth McDaniel*

Owens Market, circa 1948, owned by George Moore and Thomas Steppe. *Submitted by Jean Graham*

Ambar Store. Leah Ann Allen Clift, standing by the well. Matt Clift is wearing a white shirt. *Submitted by Mary Ann Cameron*

Chapter 4: Making a Living 53

Weedonville Store and Post Office. *Submitted by Betty Lou Braden*

Shiloh Store and Post Office. *Submitted by Betty Lou Braden*

Once the home and store of Thomas Balwin Harris and Son, in recent years used by the Jaycees as a "Haunted House." *Submitted by Elizabeth Lee*

Weldon Store on Route 301 flourished in the era following the completion of the James Madison Bridge and the Potomac River Bridge. *King George County Museum*

Post office at Igo opened in 1893. Charles T. Purks was the first postmaster. Photo, early 1900s. *Submitted by Mary Ann Cameron*

Index Store, or Parker's Store, operated as a store until the 1970s. Photo taken by Ralph E. Fall, 1971. *Virginia Department of Historic Resources*

54 *King George County: A Pictorial History*

Thomas B. Harris and wife Annie King Harris in their store, Comorn, circa 1930. *Submitted by Marjorie Morse*

DeShazo's Store on Route 3 at Lamb's Creek Church Road. This building was an operational store until the eastbound lanes of Route 3 were constructed. *Submitted by Betty Lou Braden*

Circle Market, on Route 301 in Edgehill. Left to right: Mr. L. V. Clare and Mr. W. W. Clare. 1947. *Submitted by Dixie Washington*

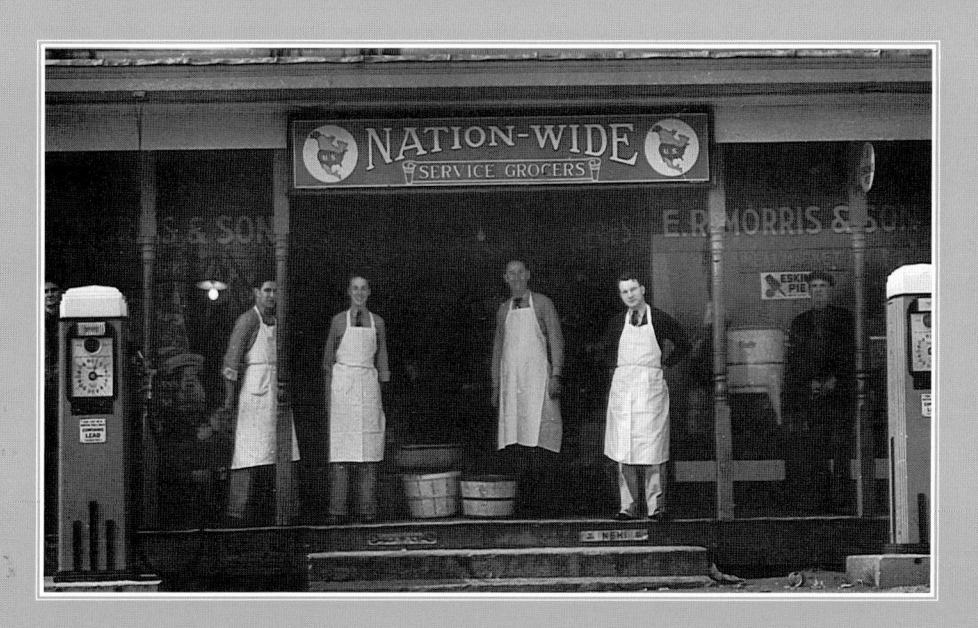

Courthouse Market, built and operated by Elmer Morris, Sr. Before this store was built, a small frame store operated by Wyatt Minor stood at the corner of Route 3 and the entrance to the courthouse. This first store was converted to a barbershop, operated by Horace Staples and, later, Judson Newton. Morris's store was later operated by Willard Garner and was often referred to as Garner's Store. Left to right: Unidentified man; James R. "Happy" Morgan; Elmer Morris, Jr.; Elmer Morris, Sr.; Willard Garner; and unidentified man. *Submitted by Elmer Morris, Jr.*

Top left: Hotel, shown on early plats of the King George Courthouse area. It was an active hotel into the twentieth century. In the 1930s, the basement was converted into a beauty parlor, operated by Virginia McDaniel and Margaret Harris Clift, and is believed to be the first beauty salon in the county. *Submitted by Betty Lou Braden*

Top right: King George Hotel. The hotel was located next to the Morris Store at King George Courthouse. *King George County Museum*

Bottom: Circle Inn, on Route 301 in Edgehill. Photo, circa WWII, shows L. V. Clare behind the counter. *Submitted by Dixie Washington*

— THE CIRCLE —

When Route 301 was first developed, there was a traffic circle at the intersection of Route 301 and Route 205. Today, this area is referred to as "the Circle." In the early 1950s, seeing the value of a convenient place to stop on the way to the beaches and gambling casinos at Colonial Beach, Mr. L. V. Clare built a shopping strip. Prominent features were the market and a restaurant. The market was the first "supermarket" in the county.

— The Navy Moves In —

On January 18, 1918, Rear Admiral Ralph Earle, chief of the Bureau of Ordnance, because of the increase in safety hazard situations at the Naval Proving Ground, Indian Head, Maryland, made a report to the House of Representatives Committee on Naval Affairs concerning the state of the various ordnance facilities. He stressed the importance of testing heavy guns fully loaded without the limitations imposed by the range at Indian Head. He recommended that a separate proving ground be located in Virginia adjacent Machodoc Creek.

On April 26, 1918, Congress passed an act authorizing the president to take over the land by presidential proclamation and, in June 1918, the land was obtained between Machodoc Creek and Lower Cedar Point Light on the Potomac River. It encompassed the lands of Rousby P. Quesenberry, Joseph Johnson and his son King David, Lilla and Patterson Bayne, Benjamin C. Grymes, John Berry, and James A. Arnold. In June 1919, Blackistone Island, located downriver from the proving ground, was acquired.

On October 16, 1918, the Lower Station of the Indian Head facility began its role as a proving ground with the successful firing of the seven-inch, forty-five-caliber, tractor-mounted gun. It was not until 1921 that the area was named Dahlgren for Rear Admiral John Adolphus Dahlgren, the father of modern ordnance and gunnery.

In 1939, Congress approved an act to obtain more land for the naval base. This land encompassed the area from Gambo Creek to Route 614 and included a large tract belonging to the Faith and Hope Society. Many families were displaced in this acquisition.

Dahlgren now has a land area of 4,300 acres that includes several miles of Potomac shoreline and a twenty-mile downriver range for projectile testing.

The new proving ground remained under the jurisdiction of Indian Head until July 1, 1932.

During World War II, Dahlgren was mainly a proof and testing area. Very little research and development was done. However, Dahlgren personnel were involved with small parts of the Manhattan and Elsie research projects to develop the atomic bomb.

Large-scale computers were brought to Dahlgren in 1955. With the arrival of the first computer, research and development acquired a larger role, bringing scientists and

Aerial view of Naval Proving Ground, 1921–1923. *U.S. Navy*

Chapter 4: *Making a Living* 57

"Boomtown," housing area for civilians on the Naval Proving Ground. *U.S. Navy*

Above left: Main Battery, looking toward the Potomac River, 1921. *U.S. Navy*
Above right: August 27, 1945. Main Battery, Powder Section. Front row, left to right: George Leake, Betty Williams, Ethel Allison, Emma Harrison, Caroline Huff, Nellie Acors, Edna Strother, Katherine Barker, Zola Sorrell, Mrs. Marders, Russell Dawson, Earl Wilkins. Second row, left to right: Raymond Wilkins, Mrs. Haynie, Mrs. Self, Gertrude Zorn, Betty Nuckols, Mrs. Perry, Mrs. Bay, Mrs. Clift, Bernice Sullivan, Mrs. White, Louise Fitzhugh, Mrs. Lee, Ester Gattrell. Third row, left to right: Ltjg. Haar, Joe Ayers, Lew Rollins, Mr. Griffin, Richard Gray, Mac Brown, Jessie Davis, Mr. Mullen, Ed Jennings, Daniel Filmore, Robert Dawson, Charles Peyton, Lt. Fisher. Back row, left to right: Lt. Pinker, T. F. Wilkins, Mr. Cheatham, Nelson Ferrell, Archie Dodson, Tom Washington, Mr. Sanders, Mr. Posey, Fred Burrell, Roy Coghill, Cleveland Gray, Willie Johnson. *U.S. Navy*

engineers to the area. Originally housed on the base, employees had very little interaction with the community. As the area grew and on-base housing for civilian employees was slowly phased out, the scientific and engineering community became a vital part of King George County.

Today, the population of the county has shifted from the farmer and fisherman to the science, engineering, and support fields.

KING GEORGE POST OFFICES
— PAST AND PRESENT —

- Alden 1875
- Allnutt 1922
- Ambar 1890
- Berthaville 1898
- Clifton 1847 *changed to* Chatterton 1865
- Chestnut Hill
- Coast 1914
- Comorn 1854
- Dido 1888 *changed to* Dahlgren 1919
- Dogue 1893
- Ducat 1901
- Edge Hill 1850
- Ferrell 1909
- Gera
- Goby 1898
- Gulvey 1902
- Hampstead 1828
- Hooe's 1873
- Igo 1898
- Index 1898
- Jersey 1903
- King George 1825
- Ninde's Store 1886
- Nocum 1908
- Osso 1882
- Passapatanzy 1871
- Port Conway 1827
- Prim 1911
- Rokeby 1910
- Rollins Fork 1875
- Sealston 1899
- Shiloh 1837
- Weedonville
- Welcome 1892
- Will 1916
- Alto 1886 *changed to* Hop Yard 1889
- Vivian 1899
- Friendshipville 1866
- Lewisville 1871
- Greenlaw's Wharf 1876
- Choptank 1888
- Hudibras 1889
- Concord 1887
- Uptonburg or Uptonville 1894
- Milville 1825
- Owens 1882
- Mathias Point 1874
- La Grange 1874
- Pluck 1894
- Rosita 1894
- Grigsby 1894
- Neill 1896
- Carnation 1897
- Scribner 1914
- Wilmont 1911

James A. Ferrell Store and Post Office on the corner of Ridge Road and Pine Hill Road. Irvin Padgett is standing on the porch. *Submitted by Irvin Padgett*

Owens Post Office. Standing are Nannie Owens, Martha Henson Henderson, and Annie Peyton Olive. *Submitted by Delores Shea*

— POST OFFICES —

Local post offices were, like the local store, within walking distance. Because of the poor condition of the roads, slow transportation, and few telephones, even in the mid-1900s, letter writing was the only means of communication. Friends and relatives in other neighborhoods within the county frequently wrote to each other.

Hooe's Post Office and Store was the first self-service store in the area. It was located at Hooe's, Virginia, near the intersection of Mathias Point Road and Owens Drive. Pictured are Joe Suttle and Jim Hoge. *Submitted by Delores Shea*

Created by Jean Graham

Left: Richard Henry Owens, postmaster of Owens Post Office. He died in 1913. *Submitted by Delores Shea*

Right: Bertha P. Reamy, born in 1887, daughter of Alexander Reamy, for whom he named the post office, Berthaville. *Submitted by Lois Reamy*

Chapter 4: *Making a Living* 61

August 1941. Top row, right to left: Cdr. H. D. Hoffman, Lt. Cdr. T. S. Parsons, Lt. H. S. Harnly, Capt. D. I. Hedrick, Lt. Cdr. C. Buchanan, H. S. Jenkins, C. B. Peters, Ed Worrell. Lower row, right to left: H. Chinn, J. B. Rawlette, F. M. Marshall, W. A. Rose, J. H. McClanahan, A. A. Rogers, E. B. Williams, J. F. White, Chief Gunner Kapa (standing), W. F. Jenkins, A. G. White, W. W. Clare, L. V. Morgan, G. B. Elliott, L. M. Fritter, George Garner, and F. B. Staples. *U.S. Navy*

August 4, 1945. Plate Fuse Battery. Front row, left to right: W. B. Lewis, W. Cleek, C. Shook, M. Rose, M. Baird, B. Wegner, N. Atkins, N. Wall, J. Owens, Ens. F. M. Perkins, Ltjg. V. Philipchuk, Cdr. C. T. Atkins, Cdr. G. K. Williams, Lt. P. A. Krentel, Ltjg. J. H. Roseboom, Grayson Elliott, H. Legg, E. Pulliam, D. Thornhill, A. Wasner, E. Armstrong, N. Sperano, D. Stone, L. Morgan, F. Staples. Standing, left to right: W. Bandy, G. McKenney, J. Daffen, H. Green, J. White, M. Henderson, W. Marshall, J. Jenkins, G. Clarke, A. Brent, T. Newton, I. Davis, G. Alford, T. Stewart, J. Nash, J. Parker, L. Newton, H. Crowley, R. Rice, E. Brown, J. Bellomy, R. Reeves. *U. S. Navy*

60 *King George County: A Pictorial History*

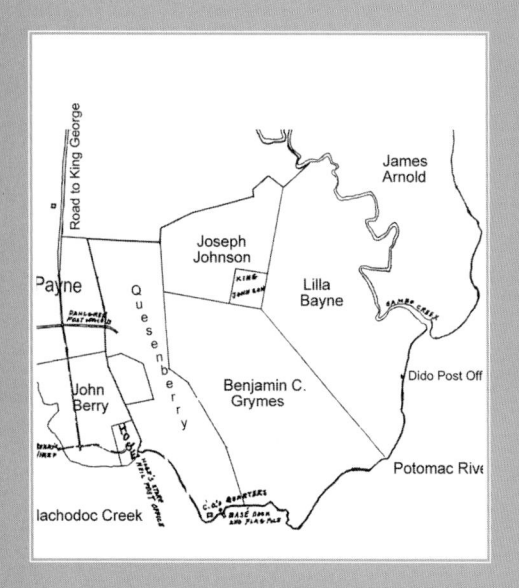

Top left: Plat illustrates the plantations and farms consumed by the Naval Proving Ground. *Revised from a plat drawn by James Payne*

Top right: First firing of 7"/45 Caterpillar gun, Dahlgren, October 17, 1918. *U.S. Navy*

Middle: First administration building and living quarters at the Naval Proving Ground, 1918. *U.S. Navy*

Bottom: View of Naval Proving Ground, early 1920s. *U.S. Navy*

Chapter 4: Making a Living 59

Will Post Office. *Submitted by Betty Lou Braden*

This blacksmith shop, owned by Luther Miller, was on the southwest corner of present Route 301 and Route 3. Circa 1910. Left to right: Luther Miller, John McDaniel, Jeff Bass, Lloyd Muse, George Grymes, and William T. Hudson. *Submitted by Carlton and Lois Griffin*

Machodoc Creek, facing present-day Dahlgren. In the boat: James L. Hoge; Caroline (Owens) Hoge; their children: Gertrude, Willard, and Granville; and Frank H. Peyton. To the right is Neill Post Office. Photo pre-1918. *Submitted by Pauline Sharpley*

Edgehill Post Office, at Route 205 and Hanover Church Road, near the Circle. It was operational into the early 1950s. Photo by Ralph E. Fall, 1971. *Virginia Department of Historic Resources, Richmond, Virginia*

Service station was once owned by Frank Hudson. Today, it stands across the road in front of the courthouse. *Submitted by Betty Lou Braden*

Clift's Garage. *Submitted by Betty Lou Braden*

Chapter 4: Making a Living 63

King George Motor Company, operated by Halsey Dickerson. The building had also once been a farm machinery business operated by Joseph A. Billingsley, Sr. From 1918 into the early 1920s, the County Farm Committee held the county fairs in this building and surrounding grounds. During World War II, part of the front showroom was rented to the OPA for use as a War Price and Rationing Board Office. In 1945, the building burned and was replaced by the Morris Chevrolet building. *Submitted by Elmer Morris, Jr.*

Oak Crest Vineyard and Winery, one of the newest King George County businesses, produced its first harvest in 1999. The wine production facility is underground. *Photo by Elizabeth Lee*

Jeter Lumberyard operated for many years at the current post office site. *Submitted by Betty Lou Braden*

Post-1945 Morris Chevrolet building. *Submitted by Bettie Lou Braden*

Cleve Packing Plant, located on historic Cleve plantation in Dogue. *King George County Museum*

Birchwood Power Plant rises over the flat farmland of King George County. *Photo by Elizabeth Lee*

Mr. Winfield Morgan plows out the driveway of Mr. Wallace Newton after a snowstorm in the early 1940s. *Submitted by Eula Mae Morgan Tate*

Bank of King George, built about 1928 with Fred Davies as its first cashier. When King George Motor Company burned in 1945, the bank was heavily damaged. Mr. H. W. B. Williams, president, transacted business from his car, parked in the church yard across the street. The building was repaired and used as a bank until the new facility was constructed across the street. The original building was used for many years by the Health Department. *Submitted by Betty Lou Braden*

Mining gravel at Ed Taylor's. *King George County Museum*

Marcellus Fitzhugh was a colporteur, a seller of religious materials. He traveled the Northern Neck in his horse and buggy. Mr. Fitzhugh died in 1906. *Submitted by Elizabeth Lee*

Charles H. Harris's Store, "Buddy's Superette," was located in Dogue. This building replaced an earlier store. *King George County Museum*

In the 1940s, Leon Rosenburg opened the Mount Rose Canning Company in King George. By 1950, it was a large business in King George. *King George County Museum*

Chapter 4: *Making a Living*

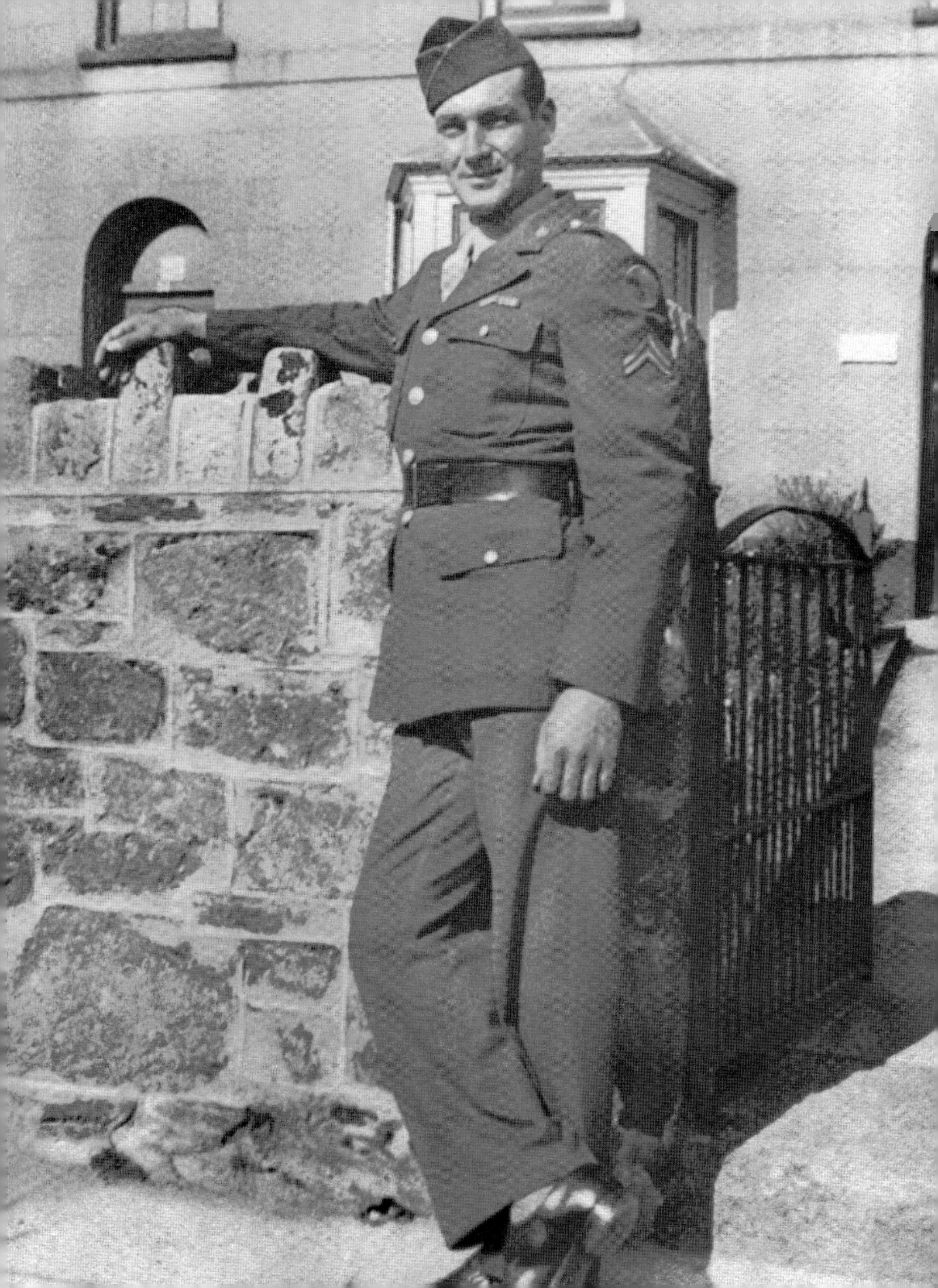

Chapter 5

When Duty Calls

— Revolutionary War —

King George County, like all of Virginia, took up arms for freedom from Great Britain. In 1788, Betsey Rigg was declared an orphan who lived with her grandfather, William Armstrong, in King George County. Her father, Benjamin Rigg, a soldier of the Fifth Virginia Regiment, died in the Continental Army service. James Baker was killed in action in July 1779 at Stoney Point. John Washington died in service in about 1778. John Lurty was a captain in the State navy. He died in King George County in 1795. Hosea Rogers, James Armstrong, James Marshall, John Cox, Thomas Gordon, Francis Conway, and Seymour Hooe were a few of those who served from the county.

— WAR OF 1812 —

The United States declared war on Great Britain on June 12, 1812. There had been a long-standing dispute with England over the Northwest Territory and the Canadian border. In 1810, the British had attacked the USS *Chesapeake*. The central dispute was over the impressments of American soldiers by the British.

As usual, King George County citizens heeded the call to war. Among those who fought were James Bailey, John Brissey, Lovell Carver, John Ferrell, John Hart, Charles Henderson, Joseph Jones, Samuel Kendall, Henry Lane, Joseph Lane, James Moss, Thornton Moss, James Rawlett, William Rawlett, Thomas Rose, William Sullivan, Benjamin Truslow, John Tyson, Lawrence Underwood, Newton Wilkinson, S. J. S. Brown, Thomas B. B. Baber, and James Lee.

— MEXICAN WAR —

The Mexican War also touched King George County. For the first time, soldiers did not need to defend their own homeland. King George resident Seymour Hooe lost three sons to the war.

— KING GEORGE COUNTY SURVIVES THE WAR BETWEEN THE STATES —

By 1860, King George County was already gearing up for war. The home guard, the Twenty-fifth Virginia Regiment, was already an active group of soldiers:

Napoleon B. Arnold, William S. Brown, James W. Burnett, John Carver, John F. Dickinson, William H. Dickinson, James Ellis, Daniel Fitzhugh, Robert Fitzhugh, Joseph S. Greenlaw, Thomas J. Grymes, George E. Grymes, William H. Gaines, F. C. S. Hunter, Stephen F. Harris, James E. Jones, William Inscoe, William F. King, Henry B. Lewis, George W. Lewis, George Thomas Lee, Thomas S. D. Massey, Samuel Rollins, John P. Robb, Jessie W. Rollet, John Rowley, E. P. Tayloe, B. T. Tayloe, Alexander W. Tennant, William Tayloe, George McDaniel, William E. Rose, W. W. Rose, William Jones, T. T. Arnold, H. Rollins, Joseph F. Lee, Edward Agar, William H. Griffin, William B. Taylor, Richard Holbert, William Owens, John Minor, James Jones, A. Broaddus Porter, Robert F. Bruce, Henry Worrell, Benjamin F. Price, Thomas Jackson, R. H. Hudson, Thomas Scott,

Confederate monument, King George Courthouse. *Virginia Department of Historical Resources, Richmond, Virginia*

Left: Charles Collins, a graduate from West Point, was born in Philadelphia. He came to King George and married Susan Augusta Mason, daughter of Wily Roy Mason, at Cleveland in 1860. He was killed in Spotsylvania on May 7, 1864, and is buried at St. John's Church cemetery in King George. *King George County Museum*

Right: John Arnold Edwards was killed in Richmond on January 17, 1864. He is buried in Hollywood Cemetery, Richmond, Virginia. *Nancy Edwards Harris Collection, King George County Museum*

Daniel McDaniel, Sandford Morgan, George W. Scott, John W. R. Jay, Stanfield Jones, James Dillard, Andrew S. Stiff, James Strother, John L. Staples, Dangerfield Pitts, Richard Pitts, W. Roberson Taylor, Major Taylor, Frank L. Dade, Ashton G. Dade, P. M. Jett.

This war, more than the previous wars, touched the civilian sector of the county. Many women, children, and elderly had been left to fend for themselves. Northern blockades made it difficult to get needed medicines for the sick. Diphtheria, typhoid, consumption, smallpox, and pneumonia claimed the lives of a large number of citizens. Salt, desperately needed for food preservation, was depleted because of the difficulty of transporting it from the salt mines.

Because of its location, King George County was constantly occupied or under the threat of occupation by Union troops. Citizens endured raids on their homes, the theft of livestock, and loss of valuables. If the children were able to attend school, they were in danger of becoming casualties of war. Joseph Perry came home after being a prisoner of war. He found his family living at Somerset and had to spend several years working off the debt acquired by them during his absence.

Those able-bodied men who chose not to fight were forced to hide. In December 1864, King George County Court records show that several King George citizens were reported either as deserters or "avoiding the military service by concealing themselves." Among those named were William E. McClanahan, John Carver, Baldwin Lee, George B. McKenney, Joseph A. Wilkerson, Lewis Jones, William Jones, Basil Jones, Richard H. Holbert, Herbert Henderson, and James Henderson. Many soldiers were occasionally reported "absent without leave." Such men found it necessary to leave the army, risk capture, and come home to plant or harvest their crops in order to support their families. Many soldiers of the Ninth Virginia Cavalry, Company I, became POWs in King George County. Among them were Joseph F. Billingsley, John R. Dickens, and Thomas P. Greenlaw.

At the March 1862 court term in King George County, it was "ordered that in the event of an invasion of the county by the public enemy so as to endanger the public records of this county, the Clerk of this Court cause the same or the most important portion thereof, to be transported beyond the limits of this county to such place of safety as he may deem best for the public interests." Rather than transport the records to Richmond, William S. Brown, clerk of the court during this time, took as much of the records as he dared to his home Waverley and hid them in the eaves of the attic.

Starvation was a constant threat to the population of King George County both during and after the war. Union troops and wandering civilians took produce from the gardens, fowl from the barnyards, and livestock from the fields. The loss of servants and the theft of farming horses and mules made harvesting large crops impossible. Raiding soldiers destroyed existing crops. It is no wonder that those who had a crop tended to hoard the harvest or to sell it to the highest bidder.

In the February 1864 court term, Charles G. Jones was appointed agent over the poor, in response to an act of the General Assembly on October 31, 1863, that entitled "an act for the relief of the Indigent Soldiers & c." At the March 1864 term, Jones reported that he was unable to purchase three hundred barrels of corn needed to supply the poor. He blamed the difficulty on the reluctance of those who had the corn to sell their surplus or the preference of selling to the highest bidder, mostly out of the county. In December 1864, Jones was authorized to confiscate corn from those who had avoided military service or had deserted the service. By January 1865, he was given the authority to take the corn from those who refused to sell it to him or to confiscate all corn being sold out of the county.

King George County saw many changes following the surrender of General Lee in April 1865. Returning from the war, Confederate soldiers found that the life they fought so hard to protect had ceased to exist. Picking up the pieces and starting over would not be an easy task.

Some fathers, husbands, sons, brothers, neighbors, and friends never returned. Virginia lost about one quarter of its fighting soldiers. Burditt Washington Ashton, age twenty-three, was missing in Gettysburg on July 3, 1863. He was one of ninety-six men who never returned to King George County. This was truly a period of chaos for King George as well as all Virginians. In 1867, the ladies of King George County founded an organization known as

Top: James Oscar Peed, born in 1844, Ninth Virginia Cavalry, Company I. He died at Point Lookout, Maryland, on December 22, 1863. *Submitted by Janet Neimeyer*

Bottom: John Nathaniel Peed, brother of James Oscar Peed, born in 1843, survived the war and lived until 1935. *Submitted by Janet Neimeyer*

the Ladies Memorial Association of King George County, Virginia. Its object was to perpetuate the memory of the gallant soldiers who had given their lives in the service of the Confederate states. To raise the money for such an undertaking, the ladies had a series of entertainment, dinners, tableaux, and tournaments. The Confederate Monument, on the courthouse grounds, is believed to be the oldest such monument in the south. It was dedicated on November 15, 1869, to the memory of those ninety-six citizens who died in the war. Some fifty years after the war, in 1912, the Confederate veterans of the county added names of others who served. At that time, it was determined that the monument had been built on the land of Dr. Thomas Lomax Hunter and that it was the property of his heirs. The heirs agreed to give the title of one hundred square yards of land on which the monument stood to the trustees for the Confederate soldiers of the county, appointed by the court. When the road was improved through the courthouse area, the land of the monument was taken up by the road and the monument was moved closer to the courthouse. The minutes from the Confederate Memorial Association of King George County, Virginia, tell us in 1867,

The war was just ended, homes were destroyed, labor demoralized, our people were deeply in debt; indeed, devastation and destruction were in evidence everywhere.

The list of soldiers killed, according to the Confederate Memorial were seventy-eight privates: R. Dishman, J. Mazingo, W. E. Rogers, R. T. Carver, H. Griffin, G. McClanahan, J. Martin, W. Warren, W. Owens, J. Griffin, R. E. Hooe, R. Baily, P. Phillips, J. Redman, C. Scrivener, J. J. Henderson, W. W. Potts, P.

Left: Marcellus Taylor Fitzhugh, although wounded, returned home to marry and raise a large family. *Submitted by Elizabeth Lee*

Above: Lovell Madison Rose, who served in the Civil War, was born May 1839 and died at the age of eighty-four in 1923 at home on the farm, now on Washington Mill Road. In the back is his son, Stephen R. Rose. 1922. *Submitted by Gloria Sharp*

Barnesfield, as it looked before it was burned by Union troops in 1861. Artwork by Jean M. Graham, copied from a frequently circulated sketch by an unknown artist.

Bowie, H. Atwell, H. Worrell, B. N. Lee, R. S. Purkins, J. G. McClanahan, J. McDaniel, L. Tricker, R. Tricker, W. Jones, J. Allen, J. L. Lunsford, N. Monteith, Y. Kennedy, J. Gouldman, J. Suttles, L. Jones, J. Lee, J. Allensworth, W. Owens, T. M. Peed, J. Baker, F. Henderson, P. Pollard, E. Ager, M. Stokes, Warren W. Worrell, J. Jones, G. W. Davies, S. Staples. F. L. Dade, T. Tricker, D. Wilkerson, W. Thompson, L. E. Crismond, J. Peed, J. Owens, O. Pursley, R. Hall, J. Tricker, W. Rogers, W. Pemberton, J. Marders, B. Portner, H. H. Howland, R. Moore, D. M. Fitzhugh, T. Bowie, M. O. Taylor, W. W. Worrell, H. Rogers, J. M. Spilman, P. Edwards, J. Frank, A. Barker, G. Barker, J. Spilman, W. Staples, A. Coakley, S. Jones, H. W. Crismond; and eighteen officers: Lt. P. M. Arnold, Sgt. M. B. Arnold, Lt. D. L. Baber, Cpl. R. E. Carver, Capt. C. R. Collins, Sgt. J. Dickens, Sgt. T. J. Edwards, Lt. H. M. Fitzhugh, Capt. H. L. Foster, Cpl. P. Hudson, Surg. T. L. Hunter, Cpl. E. Jones, Sgt. J. Jones, Surg. G. W. Lewis, Cpl. J. H. Pratt, Lt. J. Rollins, Capt. B. T. Tayloe, Sgt. J. E. Thompson.

Numerous soldiers came home permanently maimed. Many of the soldiers who did survive were disillusioned. Marcellus T. Fitzhugh enlisted in the Ninth Virginia Cavalry, Company I, on March 8, 1862, at the age of fifteen years, so anxious to fight for the cause that he lied about his age. In July 1864, he was reported as a deserter. A bounty hunter brought him back to his unit. James Jones enlisted in 1864. He deserted at Chambersburg on July 10, 1864, and deserted again from the Tenth New York Cavalry. Alvan B. Cleves enlisted in November 1861 and surrendered at Gettysburg in 1863. He claimed that he was a New York native conscripted against his will.

With the exception of the Battle of Mathias Point, no major battles were fought on King George soil. King George County, however, was by no means a sanctuary. In June 1861, federal gunboats moved up the Potomac River, shelling the Barnesfield house. Men were sent ashore to torch the house. The 146-year-old house, which had been truly a house "where George Washington slept" in 1760, was totally destroyed. On the night of March 20, 1862, Capt. Darwin Willard of the Seventy-second New York Volunteer Infantry took one hundred men and crossed the Potomac River to engage the enemy at Boyd's Hole. On April 24, 1863, a skirmish occurred near King George Courthouse. On September 1, 1863, a skirmish occurred at Lamb's Creek. The Rappahannock River was not any safer. Several homes were occupied by Federal troops. The Hooe family was forced to move into the back quarters of their home at Friedland, while troops occupied the main living quarters. Rokeby was occupied by federal troops. Mark Arnold complained to the chancery court that the entire estate of his father, who died in 1863, had been subject to "frequent occupation and unwonton ravage of military forces of the United States, and this exposure continued until the termination of the recent war." He reported the loss of one mule and two horses carried off by the army. Military forces also carried off four hundred barrels of corn from the Grantswood farm. One hundred barrels of corn, one hundred bushels of oats, and fifteen sheep were carried off from Willow Hill. At the Birchwood farm, the military destroyed three corn houses and one granary during occupation. Rails and fencing were also destroyed. According to Nannie Brown Doherty, "Every tree that could be cut down was made into firewood by our enemies, even fruit trees and shade trees. Every fence was burned and the whole land desolated." At the July 1864 court term, the statement that "in consequence of the occupation of the county of King George by the public enemy, the people of said county having been prevented from holding elections for county offices," best describes the state of occupancy. The courthouse was under occupation, and by September 1865, the clerk was ordered to "make application to the proper military authorities for the possession of the courthouse and clerk's office of the county."

As the war progressed, slaves were encouraged by the situation to escape to the enemy. John Washington's widow accused William Warner Hudson, post-war sheriff of King George County, of transporting Negroes across the Potomac River in his skiff. She and her husband had confiscated the skiff. Hudson sued for the skiff, and Mrs. Washington reminded the court that Hudson's activities were against the laws of the Commonwealth at the time of confiscation. James S. Quisenberry lost thirty-four of his thirty-six slaves before the war ended. Mark Arnold, in a later statement, complained that between the period of the execution of the will of his father and the time when the estate came into the hands of himself, the executor, "very large losses had been caused to said estate by the violence and casualties of war." He reported the loss of 33 slaves, in addition to 8 mules, 2 wagons, 1 ox cart, 1 yoke of oxen, all carried off by the slaves who "absconded to the Federal army." Dr. William N. Jett lost twelve of his nineteen slaves. Losses were so great to the citizens of the county that compensation for taxes was remitted for lost slaves.

The most marked changes for the King George County government following the war were military occupation, the increase in responsibility for the poor and indigent, and the loss of revenue gained from the taxation of personal property, that property being in the form of slaves. The Military Reconstruction Act placed the Confederate states under martial law. King George County citizens lost their right to rule themselves. Military occupation lasted until January 1870. In 1865, Mr. E. W. Mason stated, " On arriving at Port Conway he found the little village in the wildest state of confusion. Three hundred Federal troops in their blue uniforms were occupying the place."

Not only were the citizens of King George County living under occupation by the enemy, but they were dealing with a division among its own citizens. Many remained strongly loyal to the Confederacy. William Rollins, who identified John Wilkes Booth to the Federal troops as the man who crossed the Rappahannock River from Port Conway to Port Royal, remarked that he and his family were never again respected in King George County. The marriage of a young lady to a man outside of the Confederacy was considered scandalous and daughters were disowned by their families for doing so. Fannie B. Dade, a King George County woman, was thought to have been a spy for the Union, helping escaped Federal prisoners of war return to the North. Fanny, the widow of one of King George County's respected gentlemen Lucien Dade, remarried a man from the North. George W. Grigsby, guardian of Fanny's daughter, Lucia Dade, stated that she "commenced leading the most immoral and depraved life...abandoning herself to the life of a harlot."

Another strong factor in the radical changes to King George County after the war was the creation of another class of citizenry. The free population of King George County had doubled once the slaves were freed, even though many of those left the county. The responsibility of the slave owner to oversee the welfare of his property disappeared. The newly freed slaves had to take responsibility for supporting themselves. Most had never had that responsibility for their entire lives. The Bureau of Freedmen, Refugees, and Abandoned Lands had been created to help the newly freed slaves adjust to their new life. Freedman's Court was set up in King George County, led by William Colton, agent for Freedman.

An act of General Assembly was first passed on February 10, 1876, "to give aid to the citizens of Virginia wounded and maimed during the late war." Applications for aid to King George County

World War I monument on the courthouse grounds. This monument was placed by the Ratcliffe, Owens, Sumner Post No. 89, American Legion, Virginia Division, 1935. Donated by Betty McGuire Smoot. *King George County Museum*

citizens who had lived to claim the compensation poured into the King George Circuit Court office over the next several years. Among them, Arthur W. Wallace, while at Fort Harrison, Virginia, in October 1864 was struck by a bombshell on the left side of his face, a little below the nose. The wound "carried away" half of his upper jaw, half of the hard palate and the teeth of the lower jaw. Both Newton Staples and William J. Allen loss sight in one eye. Butler R. Rollins was shot through the hand at Middleburg on July 5, 1863, leaving it "deformed and useless." Caldwell A. Grigsby's physician reported that Grigsby had been struck in front of the left ankle at Malvern Hill, Richmond. He added that he was "an industrious farmer and has to work for the support of his family," but that he could not do a full day's work because of his injury.

— Spanish-American War —

King George County citizens answered yet another call in the late nineteenth century. The Spanish-American War flared to the south. Among the citizens who answered the call was Joseph Johnson, an African American businessman. But instead of being sent to Cuba, he was sent to the Philippines. Later, he would become the first African American deputy for King George County.

— World War I —

The Great War brought more tragedy to the county. By its end, the county had lost six of its own, listed on the monument: William O. Quesenberry, Cleveland K. Ratcliffe, Allen M. Sumner, Bennie Owens, Malcolm Worrell, and Beanoil Johnson. Library of Virginia records indicate that Jesse J. Monteith, Harrison Perry, and Mark Briton Wiles from King George County also lost their lives.

— World War II —

World War II was fought on two fronts—Europe and the South Pacific. The county, gearing up for war, drafted its young men into service. The first to be called up was T. Eldred Lee, Jr., of Shiloh, Virginia.

The homefront saw many changes. Everyone in the county, young and old, had to get a ration card. Items were rationed that were essential to the welfare of our soldiers. Cars were not manufactured from early 1942 until the war was over. Most 1946 models were actually enhanced 1941 models. Citizens raised vegetables in their "Victory" gardens. Many of the women in the county went to work for the first time at Dahlgren or other defense operations.

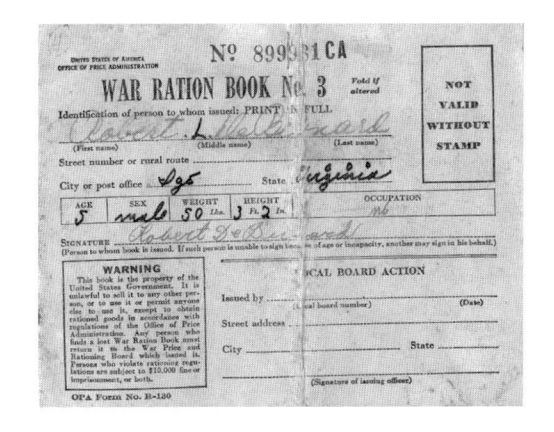

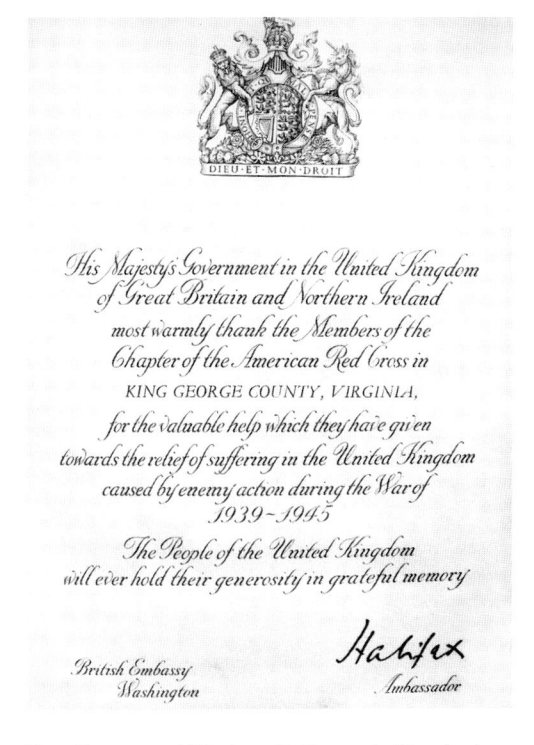

Top: Five-year-old Robert DeBernard of Igo had to have a ration card during World War II in order to get rationed commodities. *King George County Museum*

Bottom: Certificate from the British ambassador to the King George County Chapter of the Red Cross thanking them for their support between 1939 and 1945. *King George County Museum*

Chapter 5: When Duty Calls

Andrew Maurice Lee (1892–1967), World War I veteran. *Submitted by Larry and Mary Ann Cameron*

T. Eldred Lee, Jr., was inducted into the army in January 1941. He was the first draftee from King George County. Photo 1946. *Submitted by T. Eldred Lee*

William Edward Ferrell (1918–1944) was killed on the beach at Normandy, France, on D-Day, June 6, 1944. *Submitted by George and Elsie Ferrell*

Inset: Purple Heart presented to the family of William Edward Ferrell. *Submitted by George and Elsie Ferrell*

Franklin Clark Caruthers of Ferrell, Virginia, joined Company C, Second Virginia Infantry, at Warrenton on June 25, 1917. He became a member of the Veterinary Corps, ARD 309, at Camp McClellan, Alabama, on March 15, 1918. *Submitted by Julian C. Caruthers*

Billie Weedon, son of Thomas and Emma Rawlett Weedon. Photo was taken in August 1944. *Submitted by Gloria Sharp*

Estes Hudson, grandson of Marcellus Fitzhugh, in the Navy in World War II. *Submitted by Larry and Mary Ann Cameron*

76 *King George County: A Pictorial History*

Left: 1957. Twins Joe and Jerry Clift and their younger brother Donald enlisted together and were selected to attend the army's Technical Training Program in electricity. They remained together throughout their army careers. *Submitted by Larry and Mary Ann Cameron*

Middle: Douglas T. Gray III (1943-1969) was the first King George County resident to receive an appointment to the United States Military Academy, West Point. Capt. Gray was killed in Vietnam on December 9, 1969, while trying to save the lives of two Vietnamese soldiers. *Submitted by Helen Gray*

Right: Sgt. Nicholas Conan Mason, 229th Army National Guard, detailed to the 276th of West Point. He was serving his country in Iraq when he was killed on December 21, 2004. *Submitted by Vic and Christine Mason*

Those who died serving their country were Charles Carter, Robert H. Chinn, Joseph V. Farrell, William E. Ferrell, Hezekiah M. Hatcher, George S. Henderson, Leonard M. Henderson, Harry T. Herbert, Cornelius Little, Arthur Merryman, Lewis A. Mitchell, John Nash, William M. Perry, Buram D. Rakes, Doyle Emerson Armstrong, Elbert Stewart Heim, George Kelly Hooker, Harry Elgin Lee, Cleveland Madison, Henry Neukam, William Gordon Payne, Robert Carter Peyton, James Henry Prior, Anthony Salamone, Willie E. Samuel, John Wesley Scott, Joseph E. Washington, William W. Williams, and James E. Sorrell.

— KOREA —

The Korean conflict brought yet another war to our families. Donald M. Johnson and Philip T. Harrison were killed.

— VIETNAM —

William Clifton Jenkins and Douglas T. Gray III died while serving in Vietnam.

— IRAQ —

Nicholas "Nick" Conan Mason was killed while serving in Iraq during the attack on a military dining hall in Mosul.

Chapter 5: When Duty Calls

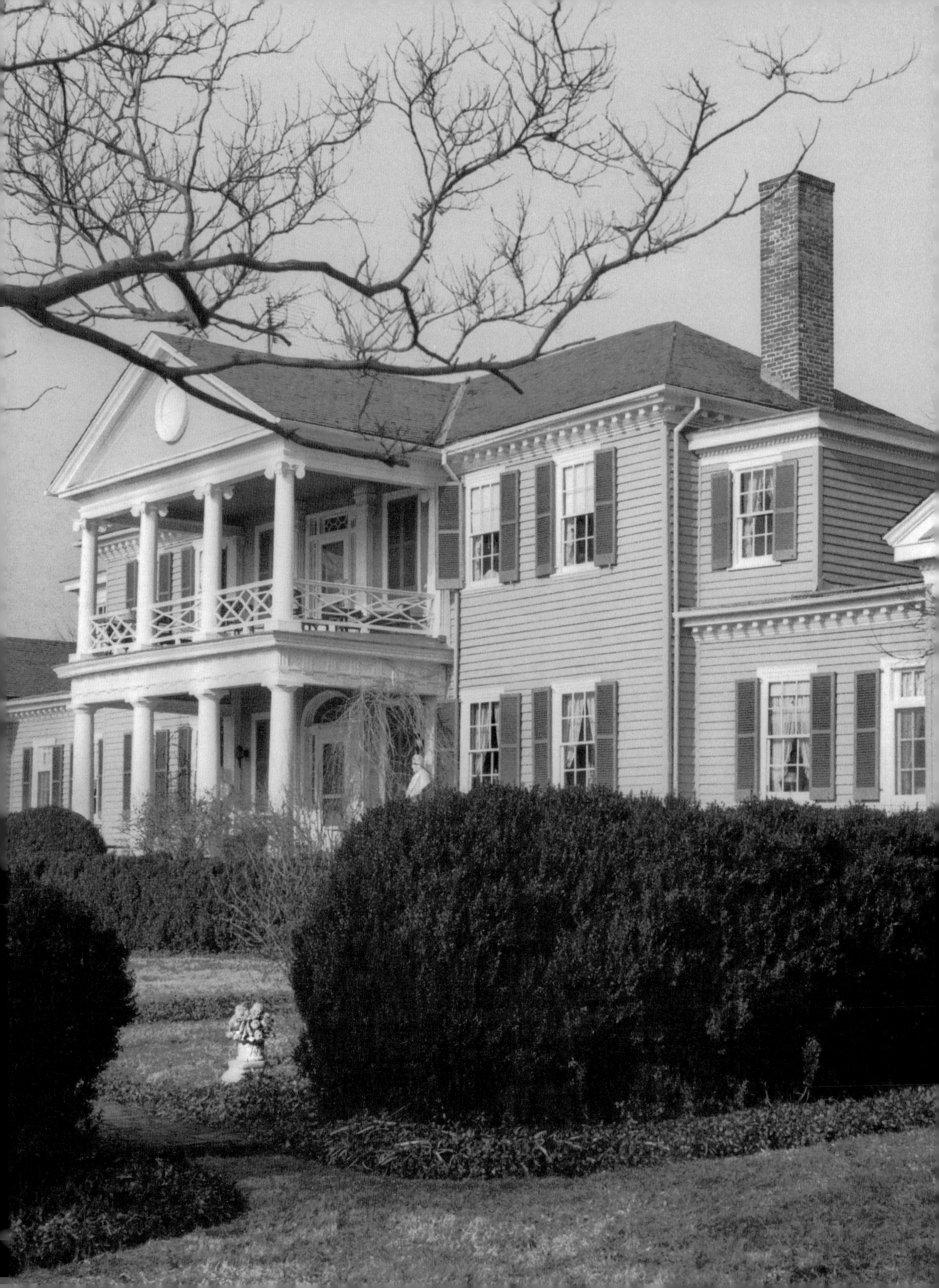

CHAPTER 6

Places In Our Hearts

From the mid-seventeenth century, homes were built in what is now King George County. Evidence of settlement in the county can still be seen today by the boundary markers placed by surveyor John Short. Because of the need for shipping access, large plantation homes were built on the rivers. Many homes have survived. The plantations did not survive. Life had changed drastically after the War Between the States. The Confederate dollar was worthless. Those who invested financially in the Confederacy were ruined. Either because of lack of money or lack of trust, the labor force was no longer there to support the large plantations. Prior to the war, chancery suits involving the distribution of large land estates to heirs suggested that the land be

Left: Boundary markers can be seen in various locations in the county. John Short was an early surveyor who marked boundaries in a lasting manner. This stone is labeled 1754. *Submitted by Janet Neimeyer*
Right: Friendly Cottage. *King George County Museum*

sold as a whole and profits divided rather than the land divided since "division rendered the land worthless." After the war, large estates were more advantageously divided into smaller farms. Those that remained large family estates were forced to use sharecropping to support themselves. Thus sharecropping became a new and profitable way of life for many newly freed slaves as well as whites with no other trade skills. A large number of plantations were sold off in smaller lots to pay debts, and a newer class of farmers was formed.

— Friendly Cottage —

Once situated on the Potomac River, Friendly Cottage attracted the attention of Captain Merrill, a Union officer stationed offshore during the Civil War. After the war, he returned and bought the house and land. The VanValzah family bought the farm in 1929. In 1932, a hurricane almost took the house into the river. Shortly after that, the house was moved to its present location on "Mule Hill."

— Marmion —

Marmion was originally built by the Fitzhugh family. One of the oldest homes in King George County, it became the home of the Lewis family, descendants of Betty Washington Lewis. Marmion is on the National Register of Historic Places.

Smith's Wharf. *Virginia Department of Historic Resources, Richmond, Virginia*

Marmion. Photo by Ralph E. Fall, 1971. *Virginia Department of Historic Resources, Richmond, Virginia*

Chapter 6: Places In Our Hearts 81

Painting of the parlor in Marmion by artist Ella Miller Hooe, 1976. *King George Courthouse*

During the Revolutionary War, Marmion's owner found a Hessian soldier wounded on the bank of the Potomac River. He carried the soldier back to Marmion and nursed him back to health. In return, the soldier, whose name has not survived history, painted the parlor. In 1913, the Metropolitan Museum of Art in New York City bought the panels in the parlor and took them to New York. The room, in a scaled-down format, is on display there.

— CHATTERTON —

Chatterton estate was patented in 1650 by Colonel Peter Ashton. At a later time, Chatterton was acquired by Henry Thacker Washington, Jr., who exchanged it with John Tayloe for Windsor. It was John Tayloe who built the dwelling.

Chatterton. Photo taken by Ralph E. Fall, 1971. *Virginia Department of Historic Resources, Richmond, Virginia*

Moreland, originally part of the Chatterton estate. Photo by Ralph E. Fall, 1971. *Virginia Department of Historic Resources, Richmond, Virginia*

— Eagle's Nest —

Situated on a high hill overlooking the Potomac River, Eagle's Nest was the home of William Fitzhugh, an early immigrant to Virginia. Records show that William was in the area about 1670. He married Sarah Tucker of Westmoreland County. William and his wife Sarah raised five sons. At the death of William in 1701, Eagle's Nest became the property of his oldest son William and his wife Ann Lee, a daughter of Richard Lee. Eagle's Nest became the home of the Grymes family with the marriage of grandson Henry Fitzhugh's daughter, Elizabeth Landon Fitzhugh, to Benjamin Grymes. The original house burned in the nineteenth century and was replaced by the present house. The cemetery has been maintained since Eagle's Nest was established, and burials include the immigrant William Fitzhugh and his wife Sarah Tucker, as well as three of their children. Eagle's Nest is listed on the National Register of Historic Places.

— INDIAN TOWN HOUSE —

Local tradition maintains that Indian Town was built by a factor of Lord Culpeper in 1650 (according to a date on the chimney) and that it later became the office and residence of Thomas, Sixth Lord Fairfax (1693–1761), proprietor

Eagle's Nest, home of the Fitzhugh-Grymes families. *Virginia Department of Historic Resources, Richmond, Virginia*

This drawing, found at Eagle's Nest, is believed to be a drawing of the earlier Eagle's Nest house. *Virginia Department of Historic Resources, Richmond, Virginia*

Indian Town House. *King George County Museum*

of the Northern Neck. A large, iron fireback from the house bearing the coat of arms of the Fairfax family, quartered with those of the Culpeper family, has survived.

The first record of the office of the proprietor being in King George County was July 6, 1737, at which time his Lordship was in King George County at his office there and signing grants and entering them in his record books. Indian Town is a typical "Virginia House" with a hall-parlor plan. Two exterior chimneys provided a fireplace in each room. The house was given to the Northern Neck of Virginia Historical Society in 1978. Eventually, the society gave up hope of restoring Indian Town and sold it. The present owners moved it to Eagle's Nest.

— Caledon —

Caledon was the seat of the Alexander family. The property became the home of Lewis Smoot, who built a more modern dwelling nearby. At the death of Mrs. Smoot, Caledon and the surrounding property, including Boyd's Hole, was given to the State of Virginia to be used as a park. Today, it is known as Caledon Natural Area.

Mount Stuart, built in 1780 by the Stuart family, was acquired by George Edmund Grymes of Monchein in 1850. *Submitted by Betty Lou Braden*

Esperanza, home of John Hill Stuart and his wife, Amelia Jane Washington, probably built about 1877. *Submitted by Betty Lou Braden*

Caledon. *Virginia Department of Historic Resources, Richmond, Virginia*

Cedar Grove, home of the Foote and Stuart families. *Virginia Department of Historic Resources, Richmond, Virginia*

— Cedar Grove —

Cedar Grove, formerly called Salisbury, was a Foote home. In 1750, William Stuart, son of David Stuart (the immigrant and rector of St. Paul's Parish), married Sarah Foote and became the master of the estate. Built by his grandson, Dr. Richard H. Stuart, in about 1840, the present manor house replaced a former building on the property.

— Litchfield —

The Litchfield dwelling was built about 1802 by Langhorne Dade. The Dade family owned it until 1852, when it was sold to James Arnold. It was James Arnold that sold a portion of the estate to St. Paul's Church in 1857.

Hylton, once part of Litchfield, was established by the sons of Lawrence Washington, the immigrant. George Washington, in 1768, dined with his brothers John Augustine and Charles as the guests of John Washington. Photo taken by Ralph E. Fall, 1971. *Virginia Department of Historic Resources, Richmond, Virginia*

Litchfield, home of the Dade and Arnold families. *Submitted by Betty Lou Braden*

Woodstock, 1969. Photo by C. Loft. *Virginia Department of Historic Resources, Richmond, Virginia*

Liberty was first built between 1795 and 1800 by John Stuart. His only child, daughter Caroline Homoselle Stuart, married first John Stith and secondly George Mason Graham. This family owned Liberty well into the twentieth century. *Submitted by Josette Gleason*

— Cleydael —

Located in King George County, Virginia, Cleydael is a Virginia landmark and is on the National Register of Historic Places for two reasons: General Robert E. Lee's daughters, Annie and Agnes, lived there with their Stuart cousins during the summer of 1861, and Cleydael was visited by Lincoln assassin John Wilkes Booth during his attempt to escape.

Originally called Neck Quarter, the three-thousand-acre plantation was purchased by Dr. Richard Henry Stuart in 1845 from his neighbor Nathaniel Hooe and was renamed Cleydael for the ancestral castle of Mrs. Stuart's mother in Belgium.

The Stuarts owned a large plantation on the Potomac River, Cedar Grove, but a malaria epidemic inspired them to build a summer home at Cleydael to

Top: Cleydael, built in 1859, was the home of Dr. Richard Stuart. This 1937 photo was taken before any restoration. *King George County Museum*

Bottom left: Hobson, 1790. *John Hunter Collection, King George County Museum*

Bottom right: Once part of Bedford, Clarence overlooks Dahlgren. Built in about 1800, the earliest records indicate that it was the home of Drury Bolling Fitzhugh in 1867. *Submitted by Betty Lou Braden*

avoid mosquitoes and humidity. Built in 1859 by slave artisans, Cleydael is living testimony to their skills.

During the War Between the States, Cleydael became the Stuarts' main residence. Dr. Stuart decided the family would be safer there as Yankee gunboats were patrolling the Potomac. Despite the Stuarts' considerable wealth and property, they experienced much hardship during the Civil War era. When John

Wilkes Booth and accomplice David Herold showed up on their doorstep seeking food, shelter, and medical attention, Dr. Stuart was aware that the Lincoln assassins were at large and was in no mood to court further trouble. He fed them dinner but refused to provide lodging. Booth wrote Dr. Stuart a note criticizing him for not doing more, which proved that Dr. Stuart was not implicated in aiding the escape.

Cleydael remained in the Stuart family until 1918 and was owned by the Richardson family until 1976. In 1986, the Cleydael Limited Partnership acquired the property and restored the house, reserving twelve acres for the historic farmhouse, with the rest developed as one- to nine-acre homesites.

— HOBSON —

Hobson was built about 1790 and was the home of the William Algernon Dade Ashton family. The original house was clapboard until the 1960s, when brick from Panorama was used to restore it. Two mulberry trees in the yard probably predate the house. In the mid-1600s, the Crown encouraged Virginia landowners to grow mulberry trees in hopes of establishing a silk industry in Virginia. Lewis Ashton and his bride, Mary Barnes Hooe, were married in 1870 and made Hobson their home.

Belle Isle, 1955. *Virginia Department of Historic Resources, Richmond, Virginia*

Buena Vista (north). Photo was taken in 1971 by Ralph E. Fall. *Virginia Department of Historic Resources, Richmond, Virginia*

Windsor was once part of Society Hill. It was built in about 1830 by Henry Thacker Washington, Jr., a cousin of George Washington. He had exchanged Chatterton with John Tayloe and brought his new bride, Virginia Grymes, to Windsor. Photo taken by Ralph E. Fall, 1971. *Virginia Department of Historic Resources, Richmond, Virginia*

— SPY HILL —

Spy Hill is believed to have been built in 1734, as indicated by a piece of iron from one of the fireplaces. The land was first purchased by John Washington, the first Washington to come to Virginia from England. He was the great-grandfather of George Washington. By 1675, he left his land to his son Lawrence, George's grandfather. Lawrence acquired additional land adjoining it, making his holdings all the land on the Potomac River between Upper Machodoc and Rosier's Creek. In 1698, Lawrence gave the land to his son John, who gave it to his son Henry Washington. Henry was George Washington's first cousin. His son, Thacker Washington, inherited it sometime after Henry's death in 1763. In 1798,

Thacker willed Spy Hill to his two sons, Henry Thacker and Warner Washington. It eventually fell solely into the hands of Henry Thacker Washington, and in 1826 it was willed to his four children: Henry Thacker, Cecelia, Amelia Stith, and Putnam Stith Washington. In 1828, it passed out of the Washington family into the Baber family when Putnam S. Washington conveyed it to Thomas B. B. Baber. Col. Baber was an early sheriff of the county. After the death of his only son at Sharpsburg in 1862, he passed it on to his daughter, Emma Baber, who married Thomas Stuart Garnett. Her son, Henry Thomas Garnett, then married Belle Brown, daughter of the clerk of court, William S. Brown. Henry T. Garnett himself was, for years, enrolling clerk for the Virginia House of Delegates. Today, the farm remains in the family.

— Stony Point —

Landon Carter was the early owner of the plantation Round Hill in King George County. It consisted of lands later known as Spy Hill, Morengo, and Mount Mariah. The early Hanover Parish was seated at Round Hill.

In 1806, Henry Alexander Ashton, son of John Ashton, willed to his son George Dent Ashton the home place containing 973 acres from several purchases. These 973 acres were later called Mount Mariah.

In January 1844, Daniel Coakley and his wife Nancy sold to George D. Ashton one hundred acres of land, originally a part of Morengo. In August 1848, Thomas B. B. Baber purchased in parts Mount Mariah from the heirs of George D. Ashton, including the one hundred acres from Daniel Coakley. This property was added to the Spy Hill tract and remained so until Spy Hill was divided among the heirs of Emma Garnett. At this time, the southeastern tract was named in the court records as Stoney Point.

Left: Spy Hill, home of the Washington, Garnett, and Baber families. *Submitted by Betty Lou Braden*
Right: Stony Point. *Submitted by Ruth Taliaferro*

Chapter 6: Places In Our Hearts

— Waterloo —

Waterloo was formerly called Chotank. Chotank was patented in 1653 by Richard Townshend, who passed it down to his son Robert. It was acquired by John Washington at his marriage in 1686 to Robert Townshend's daughter Mary. When Mary died in 1727 (John Washington had already died in about 1720), she willed it to her son, John Washington, who in 1742 willed it to his son Lawrence. The original dwelling is gone. George Washington's father, uncle, and aunt spent their childhood days at Chotank. George Washington himself spent many occasions in his youth and manhood at Chotank.

— White Hall —

White Hall was first owned by the Reverend James Wishart, first rector of Lamb's Creek Church. He died in 1774, and his widow married Michael Wallace. White Hall at this time became a Wallace home until 1902, when it was sold to Mrs. J. B. Mullen.

Above left: Marengo was an early home of Caleb Smith. Former governor of Virginia William "Extra Billy" Smith was reported to have been born here. *Submitted by Betty Lou Braden*

Above right: White Hall, 2006. *Submitted by Elizabeth Lee*

Bottom: Friedland was built by Alexander Seymour Hooe as a summer home for his family. Friedland passed to the children of Alexander's son, George Mason Hooe. At the beginning of the War Between the States, the family moved to Friedland with their cousin, Dr. Abram Barnes Hooe. *Drawing by Nancy Moore Neumayer*

Comorn House. *King George County Museum*

Strawberry Hill, home of Dr. John Minor. *King George County Museum*

Green Heights was the home of the Hansford family. *Submitted by Elizabeth Lee*

Osso. *King George County Museum*

Chapter 6: *Places In Our Hearts* 95

— Nanzatico —

Named for the Indian tribe in that area, Nanzatico was built about 1830 by George Turner. Having no heirs, George gave Nanzatico to his only surviving brother, Carolinus Turner of Belle Grove. Carolinus willed it to his son, George Turner. It was later owned by the Taylor and Rollins families. Nanzatico is listed on the National Register of Historic Places.

— Oaken Brow —

Oaken Brow was built about 1830 by Charles Taylor. It was named Oaken Brow because it was situated on the brow of a hill in a grove of oaks overlooking large fields that spread toward the Rappahannock River. In 1924, the original house burned. Soon thereafter, the present mansion was erected on the original foundation, using some of the original bricks. This three-story house is square

Nanzatico. *Virginia Department of Historic Resources, Richmond, Virginia*

Oaken Brow. *Photo by Elizabeth Lee*

Wood Grove was built on the property "Racket Hall," owned by James Edwards and his wife, Rosa Wren. Their daughter Elizabeth married John Baker in 1815. Wood Grove then became the home of the Baker family. *Virginia Department of Historic Resources, Richmond, Virginia*

96 *King George County: A Pictorial History*

Woodlawn. *Virginia Department of Historic Resources, Richmond, Virginia*

with two wings. It has four large chimneys and a slate-covered, hipped roof. The house contains fifteen rooms.

— Woodlawn —

Woodlawn was the eastern portion of Walsingham estate given to Richard Turner's younger son in 1826. Built in about 1830, this fine mansion overlooks the Rappahannock River. Woodlawn is listed on the National Register of Historic Places.

— Belle Grove —

Belle Grove, which lies a few hundred yards west of James Madison's birthplace, was originally built in the 1700s. The property was owned by the Conway family, who laid off the port town of Port Conway in 1785. It was then owned by the Bernard family and the Turner family. In about 1851, Carolinus Turner built the present building. Many believe that James Madison was born in this house. However, the major portion of the house was built one hundred years after Madison's birth.

Belle Grove, Port Conway. Belle Grove is on the National Register of Historic Places. *Virginia Department of Historic Resources, Richmond, Virginia*

Millbank is on the National Register of Historic Places. *King George County Museum*

One of several homes and businesses located at Port Conway. Some were still visible in 1963 when the southbound lane of Highway 301 was cut through the area. *King George County Museum*

Left: Cleve was built in 1729. Photo is dated pre-1917. *Virginia Department of Historic Resources, Richmond, Virginia*
Right: This drawing of the original house at Cleve was displayed on a 1775 deed. It clearly shows the hip roof. *King George Courthouse*

— Millbank —

Three homes were built on the Millbank property. The latest one is the only home to survive. Millbank was the early home of the Strother family. John Skinker acquired the property, and it became the home of Augustine Fitzhugh, his wife, Mary Skinker, and their children. Millbank is listed on the National Register of Historic Places.

— Cleve —

Cleve was built in 1729 by Charles Carter, grandson of Robert "King" Carter. At the death of Charles, it was given to his son, John Carter, who died without heirs. At this time, it became the home of John's brother, Landon Carter, who raised his family there. In 1800, Cleve was partially destroyed by fire. An early deed with a drawing of Cleve depicts a hipped roof. In 1852, the heirs of St. Leger Landon Carter, Landon's son, sold it to Henry Byrd Lewis, a son of Daingerfield Lewis of Marmion. It was again ravished by fire in 1917 and rebuilt in 1923. Cleve was long noted for its distinct symmetry.

— Berry Plain —

Berry Plain, an active plantation in the eighteenth and nineteenth centuries, was situated in Richmond County prior to the formation of King George County in 1720. It was part of the dowry of Margaret Doughty at the time of her marriage to William Berry in 1665.

The house was built in the first quarter of the 1700s. Court records show that, in 1720, Joseph Berry, grandson of William, applied to the courts for permission

Left: Celtwood, known as the Baker House, was the home of Bettie Rollins Baker and her husband, William E. Baker. *Photo by Elizabeth Lee*
Right: Powhatan. Photo taken in 1991. *Virginia Department of Historic Resources, Richmond, Virginia*

"to run an ordinary at his home place." This same Berry also operated a ferry across the Rappahannock River to Skinker's Neck, Caroline County, Virginia, in 1730. Joseph's grandson Thomas married Elizabeth Washington, daughter of John and Mary Massey Washington, in 1758. Elizabeth was a first cousin of George Washington.

The plantation remained in the Berry family until 1845, when Lawrence Berry, grandson of Thomas, sold it to John Dickinson of Caroline County. John Dickinson married Virginia Saunders of Wheatland, Essex County, and brought her to Berry Plain. The family remained in residence until 1959. Members of the Dickinson family are buried in the cemetery.

Left: Berry Plain, home of the Berry and Dickinson families. *Photo by Gloria Sharp*
Center: Dogue House was the home of William Rollins and his family. *King George County Museum*
Right: Cherry Point, on the Rappahannock River, was the seat of Daniel McCarty Fitzhugh, son of John and Alice Thornton Fitzhugh of Bellaire in Stafford County. *King George County Museum*

This house is located across the road from the courthouse. *Virginia Department of Historic Resources, Richmond, Virginia*

Left: Mount Ida. *John Hunter Collection, King George County Museum*
Right: Lothian, formerly called Pecks, was the home of the Coghill family. *Virginia Department of Historic Resources, Richmond, Virginia*

— POWHATAN —

Powhatan overlooks the Rappahannock River. During the War Between the States, it was used as a headquarters for Union troops. Much of the furniture was destroyed, the paintings were slashed, and the silver stolen. Powhatan was built in the early 1800s by Edward Thornton Tayloe, son of John Tayloe and his wife Anne Ogle, daughter of Maryland governor Benjamin Ogle. Powhatan has become the home of the family of Raymond Guest, former ambassador to Ireland. Powhatan is listed on the National Register of Historic Places.

Top: White Plains, 2005. *Submitted by Elizabeth Lee*

Bottom left: Cherry Green, home of the Welch family. *Drawing by unknown artist*

Bottom right: Edgehill was built in 1861 by Robert and Isabella Pierce. It became the home of Robert Mothershead and his wife in 1898. Twelve children were born here. *Photo by Elizabeth Lee*

— White Plains —

White Plains was built about 1725, probably by the Thornley family. It remained in the Thornley family until 1836, when it was sold to James Quisenberry. In about 1875, Alexander B. Gouldman bought the property. The house sits on a hill overlooking the Rappahannock River. It boasts a duck pond that is fed by the Gincoteague Creek, which crosses the highway at this point.

Ashland. Photo by Ralph E. Fall, 1971. *Virginia Department of Historic Resources, Richmond, Virginia*

Baker House at Edgehill. Home of the Baker and Cleek families. Now used as an apartment building. *Photo by Elizabeth Lee*

Rokeby (south) was built about 1845. When Gustavus Wallace died in 1845, it was given to his son Robert. During the Fredericksburg campaign in 1862, General Ambrose Burnsides made Rokeby his headquarters. At Robert's death, Rokeby went to his sister, Elizabeth Wallace Nalle, who immediately sold it. *Submitted by Betty Lou Braden*

Shelbourne was built in the mid-1800s. Originally part of the Wallace estate, it was the home of Judge John E. Mason and noted author and playwright Paul Kester. In later years, it has become a shelter called Emmaus for girls. *Virginia Department of Historic Resources, Richmond, Virginia*

Bleak Hill was a Thornton home. It was also the antebellum home of the Dade family. From its position high on the hill, a great view of the Rappahannock River is visible. *Submitted by Betty Lou Braden*

Mountain View, home of the Taylor family. *Photo by Elizabeth Lee*

Chapter 6: Places In Our Hearts 103

Arcadia, also known as Sunnyfield, the site of the future King George County High School. *Virginia Department of Historic Resources, Richmond, Virginia*

Farley Vale, built about 1862. Photo by Ralph E. Fall, 1972. *Virginia Department of Historic Resources, Richmond, Virginia*

Burnley is the home of the Taylor family. *King George County Museum*

Spring Hill was believed to be the home of patriot Joseph Jones, the uncle of James Monroe, and later the home of Lucien Dade and his wife Fanny. Photo taken in 1972 by Ralph E. Fall. *Virginia Department of Historic Resources, Richmond, Virginia*

Locust Dale, home of the Potts and Coakley family. *Photo by Elizabeth Lee*

Alto, the home of the Charles Mason family. Photo taken in 1941. *Virginia Department of Historic Resources, Richmond, Virginia*

104 *King George County: A Pictorial History*

The home of Dr. Veola Caruthers (1853–1929), a prominent doctor in the county. *Photo by Elizabeth Lee*

— GONE BUT NOT FORGOTTEN —

Many of the older homes did not survive long enough to be photographed or painted. Grantswood, home of Alexander Rose, has been nonexistent for decades. Bedford, the home of Henry Fitzhugh's family, burned, as did Barnesfield, the home of the Hooe family. Albion, the Dade family estate, has been replaced by smaller estates along the river. All that remained of Mount Mariah in 1971 was a lone chimney. Ellerslie, St. Cloud, Pop Castle, Eden, Cameron, Oakland, Bloomsbury, and Hagley have all disappeared. Dissington, owned by the Hooe family, was located south of Friedland. Lauderdale, in the Price family for generations, has been subdivided many times. No home exists today.

— MOUNT PLEASANT —

Renamed Nocum for the store and post office once on the property, Mount Pleasant was built between 1795 and 1820 by Aaron Thornley, a local surveyor, on the property known as Buena Vista. It had a particular appeal to merchants and was once owned by Thomas Purkins and Thomas Payne, prominent merchants of Port Conway. In 1863, it was purchased by Dr. William Newton Jett. It was here that he and his first wife, Virginia Isabella Mitchell, raised their family, including their son Robert Carter Jett, who later became an archbishop of the Diocese of Virginia and grandfather of Governor Linwood Holton's wife. In 1874, William married Caroline Matilda Turner, daughter of Carolinus Turner. In 1890, William Grigsby purchased the dower right of Mrs. Columbia Jett, which included the house and about two hundred acres of Buena Vista. Apparently, William Grigsby was living as a tenant on the property at least ten years prior to his purchase because, in 1880, his wife's death was reported to be at Buena Vista. Grigsby's descendants remained on this land until 1988, when his great

Mount Pleasant. *The painting by V. Meads is owned by Elizabeth Lee; the drawing of the house was done by Fitzhugh Nuckols*

niece, Louise Nuckols Brooks, sold the property. In 1999, it was destroyed by an arsonist's fire. Tradition states that one can see five counties from the highest hill of the property.

— CLEVELAND —

Cleveland was originally the estate of the Fitzhugh family. Prior to the War Between the States, it became the estate of the Mason family, where Wily Roy Mason, a prominent attorney in King George County, made his home. He and his wife, Susan Smith, sister of William Taylor Smith of Canning, raised their thirteen children here, including several daughters. Cleveland became the site of beautiful weddings for the daughters, as well as for their cousins. The original house burned in the late 1800s. The second dwelling, once used as a clubhouse for Presidential Lakes, was torn down in the 1990s.

Left: Buena Vista (south) was the home of the Strother family. *Submitted by Marjorie Strother*
Right: Cleveland, home of the Wily Mason family. Photo by Ralph E. Fall, 1971. *Virginia Department of Historic Resources, Richmond, Virginia*

Top left: Old Willow Hill. *Submitted by Ann Arnold Hennings*
Above: Willow Hill, remodeled. *Submitted by Gloria Sharp*
Bottom left: Dr. Arnold's office. *Submitted by Ann Arnold Hennings*

— WILLOW HILL —

Formerly a colonial estate built in 1756, Willow Hill belonged to John Arnold from 1804 until his death in 1863. John Arnold, who was born May 19, 1782, held title to 1,956 acres in King George County, which included the present Presidential Lakes property. The number of direct descendants of Lieutenant John Arnold and his twenty children number more than five hundred. The property was then passed along to Dr. Thomas Thornton Arnold and his family. On the towering chimneys could be seen the name "T. T. Arnold" etched in the brick. Behind the two-story structure was the office building for Dr. Arnold. Part of the property included a smaller building built and lived in by slaves. The fireplace in the den addition was made using bricks from Bedford.

When the first four-year high school was built in this county in 1924, the property was described as "part of Willow Hill."

Mr. and Mrs. Veola Clare owned and remodeled the house when the original siding was replaced with brick. Willow Hill was burned in 2004.

— MONCHEIN —

Monchein, Mount Chene, or Mont Chen as it is frequently called, was the antebellum home of the Grymes family. George Nicholas Grymes lived there until his death. His son, George Edmund Grymes, sold it in 1850 and purchased Mount Stuart.

Chapter 6: Places In Our Hearts 107

Top left: Office Hall, circa 1937. Office Hall is listed on the National Register of Historic Places. *Virginia Department of Historic Resources, Richmond, Virginia*
Bottom left: Panorama, painted by Ella Hooe Miller. *Submitted by Betty Lou Braden*
Right: Ruins of Waverley, home of William S. Brown. *Virginia Department of Historic Resources, Richmond, Virginia*

— Panorama —

Panorama was named for the beautiful view overlooking the Potomac River. Formerly a part of Bedford, the estate, called Green Hill, was purchased by Richard Stuart for his daughter Margaret Robinson Stuart, who had married Thomas Lomax. Thomas Lomax built the dwelling. The home reverted to her brother, Dr. Richard Stuart, who in turn willed it to his daughter Margaret, the wife of R. W. Hunter. Panorama burned in the 1960s.

— Waverley —

Waverley was the home of county clerk William S. Brown. During the War Between the States, Mr. Brown hid several vital court records in his attic to protect them from the invading army. The house was searched several times, but the records were not discovered. In 1896, a fire destroyed the house. The home was rebuilt and later became the home of his granddaughter, Marie Doherty, and her husband, Thomas Lomax Hunter. That home also burned.

— Middleboro —

Middleboro was the home of Solomon J. S. Brown, clerk of court 1838–1845. In 1848, his daughter, Maria Louisa, married Dr. F. F. Ninde; and at Brown's death in 1862, the property became the Ninde home. The only evidence of its existence today is the small cemetery on the property.

— Walsingham —

Walsingham survives only by a vague photograph taken of troop movement in Port Royal, in Caroline County, during the War Between the States. On the Rappahannock River, Walsingham was the estate of the Turner family. In 1826, at the death of Richard Turner, Walsingham was divided between his eldest son Albert, who inherited Walsingham, and his younger son Richard, who inherited the eastern portion named Woodlawn. Walsingham burned in 1898.

— Canning —

Canning was the site of the first county seat. The dwelling at Canning was built in about 1839 by William Taylor Smith. William Taylor Smith married Columbia Turner, daughter of Richard Turner, in 1839. The building burned in 1889 and was replaced by a second building, which also burned.

— Society Hill —

No remnants remain of this old brick mansion—the Francis Thornton estate—once the scene of many social happenings in Colonial Virginia. The bricks from this mansion were taken away and used to repair walls at Mount Vernon. In the 1930s, the elaborate tomb of Colonel Francis Thornton stood under a large poplar tree.

Left: Walsingham, the home of the Turner family. This Civil War–era photo shows Walsingham across the river from Port Royal. *LOC, LC-USZ62-118364*

Right: Society Hill. *Virginia Department of Historic Resources, Richmond, Virginia*

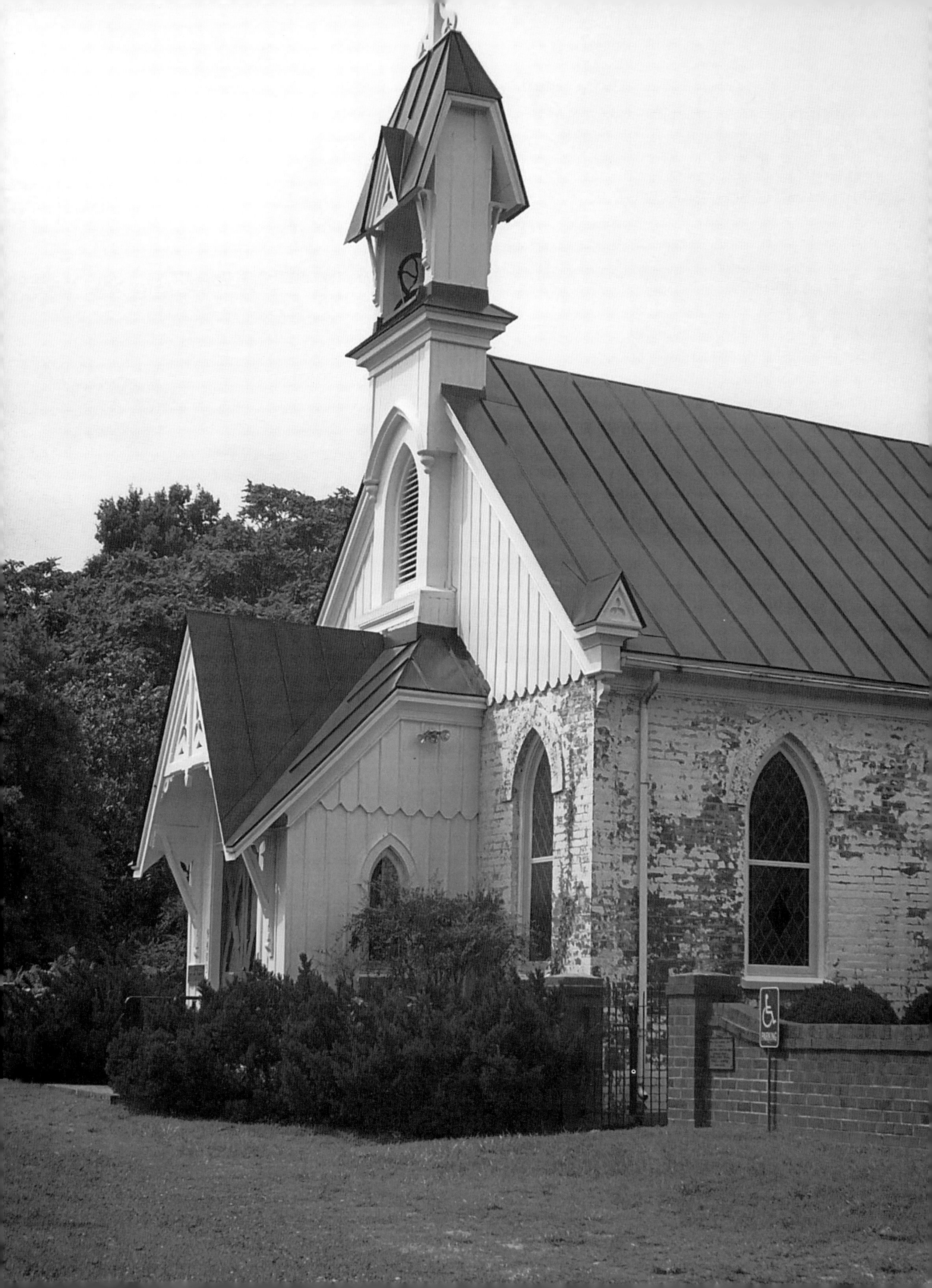

— CHAPTER 7 —

We Worship

KING GEORGE COUNTY EMBRACED THE ESTABLISHED Church of England, as did most of the Virginia colony. King George County was divided into three parishes: St. Paul's Parish, originally in Stafford County and to the north; Brunswick Parish, in the western section of the county; and Hanover Parish, in the eastern section of the county. Predating Hanover Parish was Sittenborne Parish, which was along the Rappahannock River, east of the present courthouse area. County government was centered around the church. Indeed, marriages, births, and deaths were solely recorded by the church. Unfortunately, most of those church records did not survive. Early Hanover Parish records are missing, as well as most of Brunswick Parish.

St. Paul's Episcopal Church, built circa 1766. *King George County Museum*

Round Hill Episcopal Church was located in the upper portion of Washington Parish, formerly in Westmoreland County. The only reminder of its existence is the tombstone of Mrs. Archibald Campbell, wife of the minister from Washington Parish.

St. Paul's Parish is one of the few parishes in Virginia that has surviving records of its members from 1716. This is attributed to the Reverend David Stuart, a Scotsman, who became rector in 1722. The location of the original St. Paul's Parish Church is not known, but is believed to be somewhere in the Chotank area of the county. The present building, built in 1766, is constructed in the form of a Greek cross.

Muddy Creek Church, of Brunswick Parish, was located on the west bank of Muddy Creek in present Stafford County near State Route 3. After its demise, Lamb's Creek Church was established in 1732. The present building was constructed in about 1767.

St. John's Church, of Hanover Parish, is located at King George Courthouse. Built in 1842, it replaced regular services at Lamb's Creek. After the War Between the States, the building was torn down, and the bricks saved. The present

St. John's Episcopal Church.
Photo by Elizabeth Lee

Above left: Hanover Parish House, constructed about 1752, has been the home of Hanover Parish rectors for more than 250 years. *Virginia Department of Historic Resources, Richmond, Virginia*

Above right: Lamb's Creek Church was constructed circa 1767. Lamb's Creek is listed on the National Register of Historic Places. *Virginia Department of Historic Resources, Richmond, Virginia*

building, constructed with the brick from the first building, is a smaller version of the first church.

Emmanuel Church was established in 1859. It is the third church built in this section of the county. The first was the Strother's Church, which was located on Millbank Creek. The second was also called Strother's Church. In this church, located on Gingotegue Creek, James Madison was baptized in 1751. Emmanuel Church is on the National Register of Historic Places.

— THE BAPTIST CHURCH —

Persecution of Baptist believers in the county was expected. Baptist ministers were jailed. By the revolution, the Church of England was disbanded as the established church in Virginia. In 1789, Hanover Baptist Church was established in King George County. Nearly all of the Baptist churches in King George County were formed from Hanover Baptist Church or its offspring. By 1849, the Baptist Church was meeting at three locations: Zion, Shiloh Meeting House, and the area of King George Courthouse. In 1856, Hanover split over a temperance issue, and Shiloh Baptist Church became a separate entity.

In 1820, twenty members of Hanover, Nomini, and Popes Creek churches gathered to organize a new church. It was first located near Mattox Creek in Westmoreland County and called Ebenezer. It was moved in 1850 near its present site and the name was changed to Round Hill, after the Westmoreland County Episcopal Parish of that name in the Tetotum area. In 1888, the church

Top left: Hanover Baptist Church. *Photo by Jean Graham*

Top right: Emmanuel Church. *Virginia Department of Historic Resources, Richmond, Virginia*

Bottom: Men of Hanover Baptist Church. Front row, left to right: Niven Howland, Howard Mothershead, a Mr. Brown, Walter Coates, and George Dodd. Second row: Harry Inscoe, Sr.; Mr. Berry; Julian Rawlett; Russell Mothershead; Buddy Harris. Back row: Frank Rowley, Ernest Burrell, Mr. Watts, and Kenneth Dodd. This photo was taken in the 1950s. *Submitted by Barbara Owens Howland*

114 *King George County: A Pictorial History*

Round Hill Baptist Church. *Submitted by Elizabeth Lee*

membership was so large that a new building was erected across the street from the earlier church and is the present site of the church.

Shiloh Baptist Church was organized in 1856 after a split with Hanover Baptist Church. The Shiloh faction met at Shiloh Meeting House, located a few hundred yards from the present site. Within a few years of its organization, the first church was built on the present site. In April 1942, a fire damaged the interior of the church such that the congregation held services in the Union Methodist Church building for a short time. In March 1949, a tornado tore off the roof and made the church unusable. Again, Shiloh Baptist Church congregation looked to Union Methodist Church. In October 1956, the present building was completed and dedicated.

Prior to the War Between the States and during the time of slavery, both races worshipped at the church known as Little Zion, as well as other worship houses. Hanover built its new church building, and in July 1868, deeded over the first building to the trustees of Little Zion. This church became known as Antioch Baptist Church and still sits on its original site, although the original building was destroyed by fire. In 1886, the cornerstone was laid for the present building.

Shiloh Baptist Church. *Photo by Elizabeth Lee*

Antioch Baptist Church. *Photo by Elizabeth Lee*

Antioch has been recognized as the mother church for most of the African American churches in the county.

Good Hope Baptist Church was an offspring of the all-white Ebenezer Baptist Church, now known as Round Hill Baptist Church. Prior to the end of the War Between the States, the slaves of Spy Hill worshipped with their owners at Round Hill. After the war, there was a desire to have their own church. The first place of worship was just below Spy Hill at Marengo. In 1868, Thomas B. B. Baber deeded an acre of land to trustees William Shanklin, Willis Washington, and Edmond Jackson. This land was to be used for "the benefit of the members of the colored Baptist church." At this time, the church took its name of Good Hope Baptist Church. A frame building was not erected until 1872. Under the leadership of the Reverend Zachariah Gainey, a new structure was built in 1892.

Also prior to the War Between the States, no Baptist church existed in the western section of the county. The Reverend Samuel B. Rice, a retired Baptist minister and a native of Halifax County, had married Mary Frances Arnold of King George County. He saw the need for a church in that section of the county. On March 5, 1875, Rice, Howard W. Montague, and forty-nine members of Shiloh Baptist Church gathered at Fairview School House for the purpose of organizing a new church to be called Potomac Baptist Church. Two buildings were erected to serve this church. The first was built in 1877 and was soon outgrown by the membership. The second was built in 1887.

In 1876, members of Antioch Baptist Church, wishing to attend a church more convenient to their home, established Little Ark Baptist Church in Owens. Its first pastor was the Reverend John Dunlop.

In October 1885, sixteen members of Round Hill Baptist Church met to organize a new church in Owens. After a year of preaching in an arbor near the

Shiloh Baptist Church, pre-1948. *King George County Museum*

Good Hope Baptist Church. *Virginia Department of Historic Resources, Richmond, Virginia*

Pilgrim Church. The history of the church indicates that it was established in 1838. But no records exist. *Photo by Elizabeth Lee*

This painting depicts the first African American church in King George County—Antioch. It was painted by L. Jackson and hangs in the courthouse. *King George Courthouse*

Chapter 7: We Worship 117

Potomac Baptist Church. Photo taken in 1971. *Virginia Department of Historic Resources, Richmond, Virginia*

Little Ark, circa 1900. It is believed that this might be the schoolhouse at Little Ark. *King George County Museum*

A gathering at Potomac Baptist Church, circa 1900. *King George County Museum*

Little Ark Baptist Church. *Submitted by Betty Lou Braden*

118 *King George County: A Pictorial History*

Top left: Oakland Baptist Church, pre-1938. *King George County Museum*

Top right: Oakland Baptist Church. *King George County Museum*

Bottom left: The Reverend William Windsor Owens was ordained a Baptist minister at Oakland Baptist Church. This photo was taken at Litchfield. *Delores Shea Collection*

Bottom right: Union Bethel Baptist Church. *Submitted by Jean Graham*

site of the original building, the first meeting house for Oakland Baptist Church was erected on land given by the Coakley family. This building was used until March 1965, when the first meeting was held in the present site on Route 301.

The Reverend John Dunlop organized Union Bethel in 1881. The congregation worshipped in a makeshift shelter until 1890, when the first building was constructed on one acre given by Maria J. C. Mason.

Other Baptist churches, such as Mountain View in the northwestern area of the county, People's Union, Montague, Howard's View Mission, First Baptist Ambar, Mt. Carmel, and St. Stephen's, are all offspring of the older churches. Ground has been broken for the newest church, Two Rivers Baptist Church.

Chapter 7: We Worship 119

Mt. Carmel Baptist Church, organized in 1980 by members of Good Hope. *King George County Museum*

Above left: First Baptist Ambar, organized in 1905 by Rev. Samuel J. Russell, its first pastor. *King George County Museum*

Above right: St. Stephen's Baptist Church, organized in 1873. *King George County Museum*

Bottom: Salem Baptist Church. *Photo by Elizabeth Lee*

Ferrell Chapel—an early family church at Pine Hill and Round Hill roads. *Submitted by Betty Lou Braden*

Montague Baptist Church began as a mission church of Shiloh Baptist Church in 1875. *Submitted by Elizabeth Lee*

Peoples Union Baptist Church. *Virginia Department of Historic Resources, Richmond, Virginia*

Howard's View Church in Rollins Fork was once a mission church. It is no longer used as a church. *Photo by Elizabeth Lee*

Chapter 7: We Worship   121

THE METHODIST CHURCH

Providence Methodist Church was located at the site of First Baptist Ambar. The date of the church organization is unknown, but records have been found to verify its existence.

Representatives of the Baptist Church deeded the Union Meeting House to representatives of the Methodist Church in 1829. The Union Methodist Church building was built in 1850 and served as a church until 1956. In 1942 and again in 1948, Shiloh Baptist Church held services there so that their church could be repaired. The last service was held at Union in 1956.

Fletcher's Chapel was first built prior to 1851, across the road from the present site. During the War Between the States, the building was seized by Federal troops and used as a hospital to treat smallpox victims. The building was then burned. A new building was constructed, beginning in 1894, and dedicated in 1909.

Trinity Methodist Church at King George Courthouse, also known as the Methodist Church, South, was dedicated on September 13, 1874.

Dahlgren United Methodists was formed in 1929 as a result of the growing body of residents of Dahlgren.

Above: Fletcher's Chapel, historically known as "the Methodist Church." *Photo by Elizabeth Lee*
Top right: Union Methodist Church. *Submitted by Ann Hennings*
Bottom right: Trinity Methodist Church. *Submitted by Janet Neimeyer*

Peace Lutheran Church.
King George County Museum

St. Anthony's Catholic Church.
Photo by Elizabeth Lee

— THE LUTHERAN CHURCH —

Peace Lutheran Church was organized through the efforts of two women, Bobbie Duerson and Helena Voigt, in 1963. Local Lutherans had met at Dahlgren United Methodist since the 1940s. In September 1963, the membership moved to the firehouse at King George. In May 1965, they moved into their own building, built on donated land. With only fourteen members at the time, the building was never mortgaged.

— THE CATHOLIC CHURCH —

In 1917, St. Anthony's Church, a mission church of St. Mary's in Fredericksburg, was built and remains the only Catholic church in King George County. Lumber for the church was brought from Cleydael.

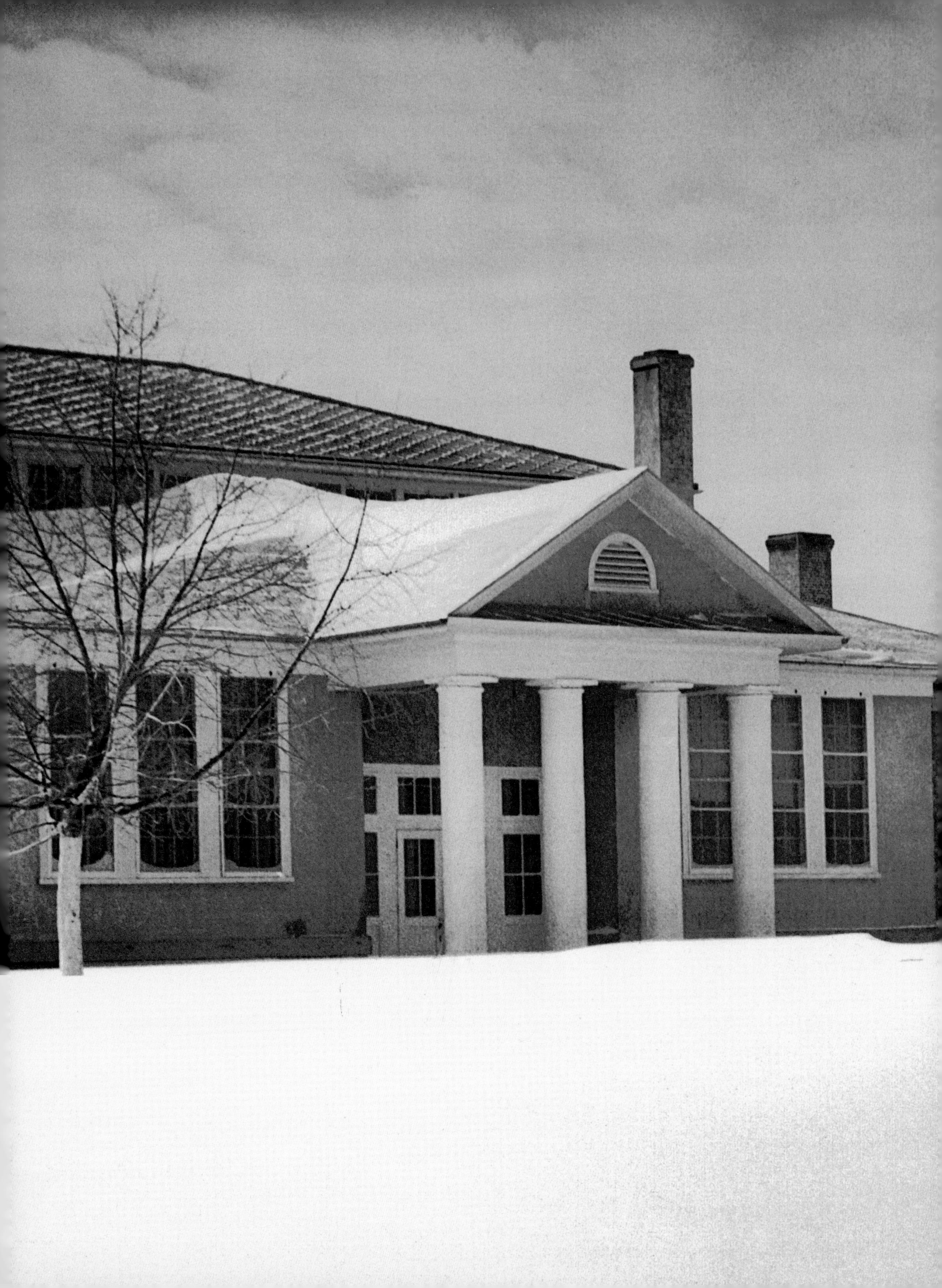

CHAPTER 8

We Learn

Prior to 1849, only the privileged could attend school. Children were sent to schools in England or in larger cities or they were taught at home by private tutors. The majority of students were male. Slave children were forbidden to learn reading and writing.

On March 8, 1849, the General Assembly passed an act to establish free school districts in King George County. A vote of the people of King George County was taken on April 26, 1849, and was accepted 242 to 20. The first board met on December 8, 1849, and consisted of Ferdinando Fairfax, Daniel Coakley, Harrison G. Howland, Frederick F. Ninde, Edward T. Tayloe, James G. Taliaferro, Stephen P. Bowen, William Colton, and William S. Brown.

Left: Lamb's Creek School. This school was used as one of the first Rosenwald schools. *King George County Museum*
Right: Passapatanzy School. *Submitted by Betty Lou Braden*

The students attending would be male and female, between the ages of six and twenty-one. Schools were established in districts where at least fifteen students were registered and a "suitable school house can be obtained without expense to this Board."

Ten school districts were established in King George County. Tuition for each student appears to have been fifty cents.

— Schools During the War Between the States —

Between 1861 and 1865, school attendees were few and scattered. Children who walked to school faced the danger of invading troops or misfired shells. Many of the more prosperous families reverted to tutors at home, if they could be hired.

— Rosenwald Schools —

In 1912, a Jewish millionaire and high-school dropout named Julius Rosenwald—the chief executive officer of Sears, Roebuck and Company—became interested in Booker T. Washington's attempts to improve the education of rural African Americans. Over the next twenty years, the Rosenwald Fund used a pioneering system of matching grants to help construct more than 5,300 school buildings in fifteen southern and southwestern states. Among those schools in King George County were Little Ark, Lamb's Creek, Prim, and Welcome.

Mrs. Olive Winston taught at School No. 9 beginning in 1905. This school was replaced in 1921 by the new and larger Lamb's Creek School. Mrs. Winston continued teaching until 1952, when she retired.

— The School Grows —

In 1925, there were twenty-two schools in King George County. This included the six-room school, which was the new high school; two four-room schools at Windsor and Shiloh; six two-room schools at Sealston, Goby, Edgehill, Little Ark, Index, and Tetotum, which was also called Madison School; and fourteen one-room schools, including those at Norman Hill, Riverview, Crosses, Sealston Colored, Ambar, Welcome, Welcome Colored, Gera, Dogue, Yellow Hill, and Prim. T. Benton Gayle stated in an interview in 1975, "Our total budget for all school purposes when I first started to work in the county was about $35,000 for an entire year."

The first school bus in King George County was operated in the school session 1924–1925 and was driven by Miss Jesse Chinn. It was a Ford with oil-cloth curtains and lengthwise padded seats. It operated from the Sealston area to the King George High and Elementary schools.

— Elementary Schools —

Elementary school was not centralized. The early school system, established in 1849, provided the entire education process until 1939, when the first four-year high school building was converted to an elementary school. Although many

Left: This painting of Mathias Point School was done by Ella Hooe Miller. *Submitted by Betty Lou Braden*
Top Right: Windsor School, 1927. *Submitted by Lois and Carlton Griffin*
Bottom Right: Mathias Point School, built circa 1890, served as the last one-room schoolhouse. It was replaced by a four-room Windsor. The teacher was Miss Maria Elizabeth Owens. *Submitted by Lois and Carlton Griffin*

Chapter 8: We Learn

Ambar School. The teacher was Miss Lelia Murphy. Front row, left to right: Earl Thomas Clift, Robert F. Clift, Mabel Clift Lewis. Top row, left to right: Pearl Clift Hudson, James M. Clift. *Submitted by Mary Ann Cameron*

Ninde, October 15, 1915. The girl who is in the second row, fourth from the left, is believed to be Virginia Elizabeth Fitzhugh, the grandmother of author Elizabeth Lee. She would have been ten years old. *Submitted by Elizabeth Lee*

Index School, 1921. Front row, left and backwards: Richard McGinniss, James Dickerson, Harold Dickerson, Tommy Bowler, Carlin Gouldman, Charlie Rogers, Thomas Pitts, Frank Pitts, James Rollins, Blanche Bowler, Glen Rollins Golden, Frances Rogers, Elsie Dickerson, Virginia McGinniss King, Louise Dickerson, Eva Bowler, Ethel Dickerson, Frances Norris, Lavalette Gouldman, Annie Bowler Marders, Rouzie Gouldman, Katie Pitts Trigger, Mable McGinniss Crismond, Eleanor Pitts, Betty Rollins, Helen McGinniss, Mamie Combs, Eva Cook, Nellie Lee, Inez Lee, Margaret Norris, Minnie Pitts Inscoe, Annie Gouldman, Louise Allensworth, Edna Strother, Audrey Olive. *Submitted by Patricia McGinniss*

Top left: Students in Rokeby School, on the grounds of Rokeby, west of King George Courthouse. *King George County Museum*

Top right: One-room schoolhouse referred to as Peace and Light School. Photo by Ralph E. Fall, 1971. *Virginia Department of Historic Resources, Richmond, Virginia*

Bottom left: First private school at Dahlgren, 1918. *U.S. Navy*

Bottom right: Green Heights School near Igo. *Photo by Elizabeth Lee*

---

smaller schools continued to operate until the 1960s, the trend was to centralize the elementary school.

When the present high school was completed in 1969, the 1939 high school was converted to the elementary school. In 1967, a wing was added to the building, which provided much needed space with the closing of smaller community schools and integration.

Potomac Elementary School was built in 1954 to accommodate the growing population of the Dahlgren community. As families moved off of the naval base, the need for a local school increased.

King George Elementary School was completed in 1997. This school replaced the 1939 school.

King George Elementary School. *Photo by Elizabeth Lee*

Sealston Elementary School. *Photo by Elizabeth Lee*

Potomac Elementary School. *Submitted by Betty Lou Braden*

Potomac Elementary School. *Photo by Elizabeth Lee*

Sealston Elementary School was completed in 2004. In September 2004, students in grades K through 6, living in the western section of the county, began the first school year.

— HIGH SCHOOLS —

The first two-year high school was established in 1916 at Shiloh. This school was converted to an elementary school and remained so until it ceased operation in 1962.

The first four-year high school was built in 1923 on part of Willow Hill property. The *Daily Star* in Fredericksburg reported on the dedication planned for May 19, 1924, as "an elaborate program, consisting of athletic and literary events during the day and dedication exercises at night." After the addition of the high school building in 1939, this school became an elementary school, with classes for students in grades one through seven. It was demolished in 1967.

King George High School, contemporarily referred to as the "old elementary school," was built in 1939 under the Federal Emergency Administration of Public Works. It remained an all-white school until the 1962–1963 school year. In 1969,

Shiloh School was the first two-year high school in the county. *Submitted by T. Eldred Lee*

First four-year high school. *King George County Museum*

King George County's first four-year high school. *Submitted by Elmer and Marcie Morris*

Chapter 8: We Learn 131

it was replaced by the present high school. Over the years, a connecting hallway was built between the elementary and high schools and housed the school library.

Ralph Bunche High School, situated near Routes 301 and 211, was once attended by African Americans in King George County. It was constructed in 1949 as the result of a federal court case that tested the "separate but equal" doctrine established by the Supreme Court in Topeka. The Edgehill Training School, which had been the school for African American students, was found inferior to the county's white high school. The training school had stoves for heating classrooms, outhouses, and no gymnasium. Students attended Ralph Bunche from 1949 until 1967, when King George totally desegregated its schools. The class of 1964 was the last segregated class of King George High School.

Left: Elsie H. S. Williams, principal of King George High School at the time the first four-year school was built. *King George County Museum*
Top right: Shiloh School second through third grades, 1953–1954. Far left, back to front: Virginia Wine, Barbara Owens, Cynthia King, Margaret Wroten; Mary Virginia Howland (standing), Shirley Parker, Kenneth Stephens, Doris ?, Gloria Shaw, Teddy Hodge, Shirley Baker; unknown, Susanne Allensworth, Jimmy Ferrell, Eddie Dunn, Jack McGinniss, Betty Stephens, Jerry Stephens; Galen Lee, Doris Staples, unknown, Mazie Wroten; Nancy Paddy (standing), Phillip Cloud, Dennis Thebadour, Joan Bradshaw. Miss Thelma DeAtley is the teacher. *Submitted by Barbara Owens Howland*
Bottom right: Field Day 1927. Christine Lee, Welford Inscoe, and Stanley Owens were identified on the float. *Submitted by T. Eldred Lee*

Mr. T. Benton Gayle, superintendent of schools, at the 1937 May Day celebration at King George High School. *Submitted by T. Eldred Lee*

Unidentified children at the May Day 1931 celebration at King George High School. *Submitted by T. Eldred Lee*

King George High School class of 1932. *Submitted by Patsy Edwards*

Chapter 8: We Learn

King George High School, built in 1939. *King George County Museum*

Home Economics and Music Building, Ralph Bunche High School. *Virginia Department of Historic Resources, Richmond, Virginia*

Ralph Bunche Student Store. *Virginia Department of Historic Resources, Richmond, Virginia*

Ralph Bunche High School. *Virginia Department of Historic Resources, Richmond, Virginia*

King George High School, 1969. *Submitted by Betty Lou Braden*

Wing added to the 1939 high school in 1960. *Submitted by Betty Lou Braden*

King George Middle School. *Photo by Elizabeth Lee*

Left: Three generations of a family with their teacher, Kate Owens. Standing, left to right: Mamie Fitzhugh Harris; her daughter Vashti Harris Clift; and Vashti's daughter, Mary Ann Clift Cameron. *Submitted by Mary Ann Cameron*
Right: King George High School was built in 1939. *King George County Museum*

Today's King George High School was opened in 1969. It boasted baseball fields and a track. King George High School continues to utilize the Hunter Amphitheater, located at the 1939 school.

— Middle School —

King George Middle School was opened to sixth-, seventh-, and eighth-grade students in 1976.

— Superintendent of Schools —

Miss Mary Harwood served as superintendent of schools in King George County until 1925. She was the only woman to serve in that position in Virginia, as noted by T. Benton Gayle in 1975.

In 1925, T. Benton Gayle became the superintendent of the newly formed school division of both Stafford and King George counties. He served in that position until 1965.

King George High School Basketball Team. Front row, left to right: Jackie Feather, John Glancey, Wayne Clark. Back row, left to right: Unknown, Walter Meade, Macon Patterson, Joe Minter, unknown, Hal Revercomb, Joe Haag, Tommy Coates, William Nuckols, and Ron Hughes. *King George County Museum*

King George ball team, about 1940. Front row, left to right: John Lee; Elmer Morris, Jr.; unknown; Brooke Mason; and Sonny Ashton. Back row, left to right: Russell Mothershead, Keith Lee, Elwood Mason, Mr. Smith, Bobby Allensworth, unknown, and unknown. *Submitted by Elmer Morris, Jr.*

King George High School Basketball Team. Front row, left to right: Walter Meade, Billy Hart, Jim Burns, Wayne Cushing, Charles Peyton, Wayne Clark, and Preston Thompson. Back row, left to right: Coach Phillips, Steve Thompson, Sonny Johnson, John Glancey, unknown, unknown, William Nuckols. *King George County Museum*

First grade, Ralph Bunche School, date unknown. *King George County Museum*

Larry Cameron, Chester Olive, and J. B. Hall plant a tree for Arbor Day at Dahlgren School, 1948. *Submitted by Larry and Mary Ann Cameron*

Ralph Bunche High School, class of 1962–1963. *King George County Museum*

Chapter 8: We Learn

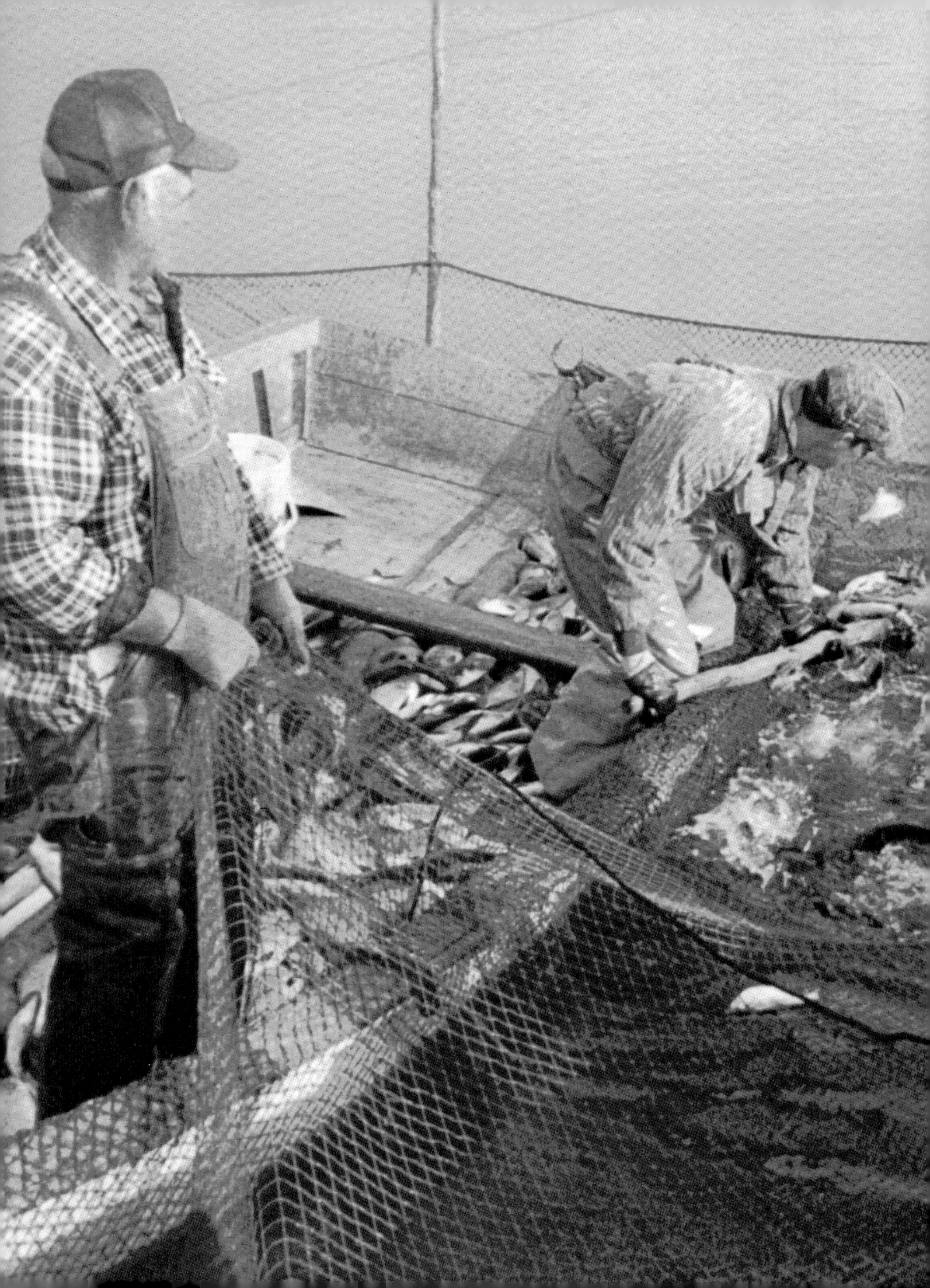

CHAPTER 9
Transportation and Waterways

WATERWAYS:
— EARLY TRANSPORTATION ROUTES —

AFTER THE FORMATION OF KING GEORGE COUNTY IN 1720, there were a number of boundary changes that resulted in the county's present size and shape, giving King George County the distinct advantage of being bordered by two large rivers—the Potomac and the Rappahannock.

Potomac Creek, named for the Indian village "Patowmeck-town," meaning "landing place for goods," borders King George for a few miles on the northwestern side. Steamboats began operating there around 1815 and, by 1837, steamers, schooners, and U.S. mailboats were in and out of the creek twice a day, carrying passengers, freight, and mail to Alexandria and Washington, D.C. During the War Between the States, Potomac Creek was an

Ernest "Capt. Billy" Green works with his son pulling up his pound net full of fish. *Submitted by the Ernest Green family*

important wagon supply base, and Army wharves were constructed of pontoons from Waugh Point to the main channel.

In 1827, a canal was proposed to run from Whipsawassen Creek (in the Passapatanzy area) across King George County towards the Rappahannock. One can only wonder what King George County would be like today if that proposal had materialized.

— THE POTOMAC RIVER —

The Potomac River channel has been mapped and buoyed since late colonial days and is shown on early charts by several names, including Patawomeck, as noted on John Smith's 1608 map. Some accounts show "Potomac" as a European spelling of an Algonquian name, meaning "river of swans." Others say it means "place where people trade."

For four hundred years, Maryland and Virginia have disputed control of the Potomac. The original colonial charters granted both states the entire river rather than half of it, as is normally the case with boundary rivers. In 1776, Virginia ceded her claim to the entire river but reserved free use of it, an act disputed by Maryland. Both states acceded to the Compact of 1785 and the 1877 Black-Jenkins Award, which granted Maryland the river bank-to-bank from the low water mark on the Virginia side, while permitting Virginia full riparian rights short of obstructing navigation.

Early King George landowners amassed sizable holdings along all its waterways. Some claimed and received land along the Potomac in both Maryland and Virginia, and many lived on or near water deep enough for ocean-going vessels. Early landowners engaged in fur trade and grew tobacco on their plantations. Tobacco warehouses were situated in waterfront areas. Ships transported furs, iron, lumber, wool, and hogsheads of tobacco to England and returned laden with needed supplies. General George Washington, in 1770, pointed out in a letter to Governor Eden of Maryland the advantages of making the Potomac "a channel of commerce" between the mother country and the immense territory that bordered on the river. In the "Annals of the Northern Neck of Virginia," the Reverend George Beale states, "Around the 1777 time period the sails of French vessels appeared on the Potomac and Rappahannock bringing military supplies, clothing, brandy, and good claret."

The Frederick DeBary steamboat docks at Smith's Wharf. *King George County Museum*

Chapter 9: Transportation and Waterways 141

Prior to the American Revolution, activity on area waterways was moderate. As time went on, locally built sloops and schooners were put into service; by the time of the war's outbreak, many people were engaged in river trade. Waterways in and near King George County provided a better means of travel than overland routes, resulting in numerous boat landings and ferries. Shipyards were developed and shipbuilding began. Records indicate that, by 1813, the *Columbian,* a flat-bottomed steamboat, was hauling wood and grain on the Potomac.

By 1837, many fisheries were located along the Potomac River in King George County, including Fowkes Landing, Eagle's Nest, and Mount Mariah. Competition in the Potomac fishing industry was at its peak prior to the War Between the States. Seines, gill nets, and pound (trap) nets were in use, and the catch was heavy. Pound nets, still used by a few rivermen, are an interesting method of catching or "trapping" large quantities of fish at one time. To set these "traps," long poles are driven by hand into the mud bottom. Nets running perpendicular to the shore are attached, and fish swimming along shore are guided towards the enclosed "pound" by this hedging.

In early years, the better grades of fish were shipped to Baltimore, Annapolis, and Washington, D.C., by fast sailing vessels and later by steamboat. Oystering was a profitable industry although the center of conflict and disagreements for generations. Oyster "tongers" and oyster "dredgers" blamed one another for taking more than their rightful share. There was also conflict between the Virginia watermen and the Maryland watermen, and the feuds were often fierce and bloody. The Oyster Wars persisted until after World War II, when laws were passed bringing these conflicts to an end.

Census records from 1860 list a few rivermen: William W. Henderson, 23, mariner; Lawrence Brannican, 52, fisherman; John A. Redman, 29, mariner; and William L. Pratt, 40, fisherman. The records determine there were a large number of slaves either working with their owners or working their owners' boats for them. After the war, almost 40 percent of the rivermen were ex-slaves working small skiffs. Many rivermen died during the war or lost their boats and were no longer engaged in river activities. In 1870, census records list rivermen: James B. Price, 30, sailor; John Marmaduke, 55, sailor; and Benjamin Shelley, 29, sailor. The census records do not indicate whether these men worked the Potomac or the Rappahannock, or other area waters. By 1880, most rivermen or their sons had improved their financial situation and were again boat owners taking advantage of the oyster and fish bonanza that had opened on the rivers.

The years between 1870 and 1920 were boom times for Potomac River boat builders. Nancies and Gill skiffs, which had been in use since colonial days, were updated due to the increase in oyster dredging. The Nancy was a flat-bottomed boat eighteen to twenty-four feet long with a square stern. It was undercut at an obtuse angle and was considered a poor and clumsy sailer. Gill skiffs were treacherous sailers and easily upset. The Potomac River dory, a larger twenty-seven-foot boat, designed about 1880, was an improvement, with a "center well" and two masts. It was an excellent sailer—fast and easy to maneuver.

This painting depicts the active roll that shipping played in our county's commercial history. Painting by Carrol Morgan. *King George County Courthouse*

Landmarks along the Potomac include Chatterton's Landing near Passapatanzy Creek, where there was an active steamboat landing. This area is where the steamboat *Wawaset* caught fire offshore, killing more than eighty people in 1883. At Stiff's Wharf, near Passapatanzy Creek, steamboats docked in the 1920s, and the wharf served both a sawmill and a tomato cannery. Belvedere Beach was a summer resort established in the 1920s; Somerset Beach boasted a quarter-mile-long pier where steamboats landed for summer excursions to Washington, D.C., from the Civil War–era to the 1930s. Charts of 1878 show it as Cottage Wharf. Stuart's Wharf and Bedford Landing were also located along the Potomac River, as well as the antebellum mansions of many prominent tidewater families such as the Fitzhughs, Fowkes, Alexanders, Washingtons, Dades, and Stuarts. Research indicates there was also a Fitzhugh Ferry.

Downstream along the Potomac, charts of 1827 show Fowkes Landing located near present-day Fairview Beach. Charts of 1920 show Smith's Wharf at this site, along with a tomato cannery, a steamboat wharf, and a sawmill specializing in "wood wagon-tongs." Fairview Beach, as a summer resort, was

Chapter 9: Transportation and Waterways

established in 1928. In 1949, slot machine gambling became legal in southern Maryland and, by 1963, Fairview Beach and Somerset Beach had a total of 180 slot machines in buildings on piers that jutted into the Potomac and thus Maryland waters, allowing "legal" gambling. In 1958, Maryland's legislature enacted a law prohibiting people from entering their gambling establishments except through Maryland and, by 1968, all slot machines had been phased out.

Boyd's Hole, now located in the Caledon Natural Area, was located on the Potomac River and was an active port for more than a hundred years. An underground spring kept a navigable channel open, and empty barges could be floated into a nearby "gut" at low tide, then loaded and floated out on high tide. Boyd's Hole was the southern terminal of a ferry to the Maryland shore. Between 1731 and 1733, Townsend Dade, Sr., and John Washington were appointed tobacco inspectors for Boyd's Hole and Marlborough. Civil War–era maps refer to "Devil's Hole" as a ferry landing in this area. A farm journal written in 1878 by Mr. Moncure, the farm manager at Caledon during Mr. W. A. Smoot's ownership, mentions schooners and steamers stopping almost daily at Boyd's Hole. These vessels included the *Matanno;* the 210-foot sidewheeler, *Jane Moseley;* and the 170-foot steamer, *John W. Thompson*. Mr. Smoot and his family traveled regularly on these vessels from Boyd's Hole to their home in Alexandria. The vessels also transported grain, wood, wool, and produce. The *Thompson* was later named *Harry Randall*, then *Capital City*, and made numerous trips from Washington, D.C., to nearby Colonial Beach.

Mrs. Anne Hopewell Smoot donated Caledon to the Commonwealth of Virginia in 1974 in memory of her late husband, Lewis A. Smoot. The Caledon Natural Area now contains approximately 2,579 acres and maintains five hiking trails, including the 3.5-mile Boyd's Hole trail. Visitors can observe bald eagles in their natural habitat. Birding, special events, and educational programs are also provided. Adjoining Caledon is the Chotank Creek Natural Area Preserve, a 1,107-acre natural area. Chotank Creek is a large, meandering creek system that flows into the Potomac River. Chotank Creek, pronounced and sometimes written "Jotank," was named for an Indian village called Acowehtank meaning, "it flows in the opposite direction." This preserve is part of the 1,431-acre Cedar Grove

Members of the King George County Historical Society enjoy hearing about the once-bustling port of Boyd's Hole, now a deserted, quiet shoreline of Caledon. *Photo by Elizabeth Lee*

farm owned by James Nash that has been protected from development with a conservation easement. These two properties protect five miles of King George County's Potomac River shoreline, including Metompkin Point, named for an Indian village "Matomkin," which means, "people who dig the earth." Charts of 1713 show this area as "Tick's Hole" and charts of 1861 show "Tompkin Point." Jones Pond is also located in this general area.

During the War Between the States, Confederate defense of Mathias Point on the Potomac River was troublesome to the Potomac Flotilla. It provided security to Confederates and their sympathizers crossing the river at this point and was believed to be a signal base in communication with Maryland. The Federal Potomac River Flotilla was commanded by Captain James Harman Ward, who was determined to destroy these batteries. On May 29, 1861, Ward, taking the lead in the steamer *Thomas Freeborn* and supported by two smaller steamers, the *Anacostia* and the *Resolute* and later by the *Pawnee*, made repeated attacks over a period of several weeks at both points, which ended with Ward's death on June 27, 1861. According to Beitzel's *Life on the Potomac*, Ward died at the hands of a Confederate sharpshooter, Andrew Pitts of Caroline County, Virginia. Captain Ward was the first naval officer killed in the war. More than a year later, the Confederates still maintained a fairly effective blockade of Washington and such vessels as got through had to endure the gunfire of the batteries on the Virginia shore.

King George County had a number of skirmishes during the War Between the States. Both Union and Confederate gunboats used the rivers during the war, and raiding parties often came ashore destroying homes and property. In *This Was Potomac River*, Frederick Tilp writes, "On June 15, 1861, a New Jersey schooner bound for Washington, D.C., ran aground at night at Persimmon Point. The next morning, Confederates, based ashore at Dr. A. B. Hooe's home, Barnesfield, rowed out and destroyed this vessel. A few days later, Union forces landed and burned Dr. Hooe's home to the ground."

In Sgt. James Scates's memoirs, *A Civil War Diary From Richmond County*, he writes,

> *We traveled up the river and landed at the Hop Yard in King George County and marching from there to King George Courthouse we camped for the night...Monday we took up the line of march for Mathias's Point, a distance of 17 miles...on June 16th, the cavalry from our regiment board and burned a Yankee vessel off Hoe's Ferry...next day we skirmished on the bank, shooting from the shore at the Yankees on the tug...all was quiet until the 23rd when the Yankees landed at Hoe's Ferry and burned his dwelling house...On Sunday we were again at St. Paul's Church and on the 27th we took up the line of march for the Hop Yard to take the steamboat...the boat ran about 12 miles down the Rappahannock where it stopped for the night...on the 28th we were 55 miles from Hop Yard.*

There were four lighthouses off shore from King George County: Maryland Point, Upper Cedar Point, Mathias Point, and Lower Cedar Point. **Left:** Lower Cedar Point. **Right:** Upper Cedar Point. Jack Lewis, the lighthouse keeper for all four lighthouses, stands in front. Photos taken in 1933. *Submitted by Mary Ann Cameron*

The newly widowed Mary D. Washington, living at Albion near the Potomac River, wrote to her mother in 1864,

> *The Yankees made a raid, killing Mr. Tennant's hogs and some of Mr. Grymes' sheep...we were in a state of painful anxiety...they have since made a raid on Potomac View...and I expect the Yankees to burn and destroy everything at this point this winter.*

In 1837, money was appropriated by Congress for the Lower Cedar Point lightship, located on Yates Bar. Nicknamed "Rolling Light," this lightship was replaced in 1855 by a two-masted vessel with one white light. In 1861, the lightship was towed by a band of King George guerrillas up into the Machodoc Creek. The Federals recaptured the lightship, but it remained vacant until 1864, when it was replaced with another lightship. In 1865, rebels again towed it into Machodoc Creek. It was towed back into proper position the next day. By 1867, this lightship had been replaced by a screwpile, white wood structure with 11.25-mile visibility. In 1893, the lighthouse burned, and a temporary lens-lantern was then placed on a platform supported by the original screwpiles. From 1867 through 1895, there were fourteen lighthouse keepers. In 1896, James A. Arnold became the keeper, followed by Frank Barnes in 1912 and Edward Speak in 1930.

In 1877, at Mathias Point, a fixed white light—visible for twelve miles—could be seen from a tower atop a beautiful, white, hexagonal dwelling. This lighthouse, located at the sharpest turn in the Potomac River, remained in use until it was demolished in 1962. Although the lighthouse was situated in Maryland waters, the keepers were King Georgians: Richard and Mary Smoot, 1876; Benjamin Grymes, 1886; Mrs. Benjamin Grymes, 1900; Charles Stone, 1908; Thomas Barnes, 1921; Bruce Pound, 1928. John C. Lewis became the keeper in 1940 and, after the light was made automatic in 1951, he continued to keep watch from ashore. In 1916, the steamer *Wakefield* sank in this area.

In 1887, the Lighthouse Board indicated a need for a lighthouse at Maryland Point, where many large vessels continued to run aground. By 1893, the lighthouse had been completed, with a flashing white light visible for 11.75 miles. In 1954, this light was changed to "auto unwatched" status. The house was demolished and, in 1963, a new flashing white light was placed on the original screwpiles. Maryland Point lighthouse keepers included William K. Slocum, 1897; John B. Fitzhugh, 1898; John E. Faulkner, 1901; Loch W. Humphries, 1905; George S. Holland, 1908; George Applegarth, 1912; James J. James, 1939; and James C. Lewis, 1950.

Hooe's Ferry, established around 1720 (some documents state 1705) by Colonel Richard Hooe, was located on the Potomac in the Barnesfield area near the present Potomac River bridge (now named Harry W. Nice Bridge). There was a charge of "two shillings per head, be it man or horse." George Washington's diary indicates he used Hooe's Ferry several times. Patrick Henry and Lighthorse Henry Lee also crossed the river in this area. In 1747, George Dent operated a ferry from Persimmon Point, just upriver from Barnesfield, to Popes Creek, Maryland. In 1813, William Hamilton was ferrying from Metomkin Point, near Boyd's Hole, to Riverside, Maryland.

Persimmon Point, downstream from Mathias Point, was probably named for a large grove of wild persimmon trees, or possibly mimics the sound of the original Indian word for persimmon, "Puchaminson." Charts of 1841 and Civil War charts show this area as Rosiman Point. There is a large sandbar at this point where boats still occasionally run aground.

At Neill, now located in the Dahlgren area, there was an active port for fishermen and oystermen, with oyster boats coming from as far as Tangier Island. At Dido Wharf, also in the Dahlgren area, there was a steamboat landing. The C. E. Davis tomato cannery was located nearby. Gambo Creek, in this same area, was named in 1691 for Alexander Gamble, a Scottish merchant. Charts of 1814 show Gamble; later it became known as Gambo Creek. Located at the mouth of Gambo Creek, Yates Point was the site of the 1920s popular summer resort, Potomac View.

Built in 1876–1877 and torn down in 1962, this unique lighthouse was located at Mathias Point. It was a hexagonal, screwpile cottage, and often described as looking like a wedding cake. The light was a fifth-order Fresnel lens. Although technically it was a lighthouse belonging to Maryland in Maryland waters, it was typically manned by King George people. *Chesapeake Chapter, U.S. Lighthouse Society*

— MACHODOC CREEK —

Notable places along the Upper Machodoc Creek (named for the Indian village Machodick, meaning "at the big tidal river") include Brick House Landing, where Francis Thornton, the immigrant, had a landing at the foot of his estate. According to 1962 writings by local historian Hugh Roy Stuart, ocean-going ships of the day sailed into this area bringing supplies from England and returning with surplus grain. Other notable places on Machodoc Creek include Little Ferry Landing, Oyster Shell Landing, and Spy Hill. According to local watermen, there were at least five landings along the Machodoc Creek, upstream of Dahlgren, where large schooners and paddlewheel steamers would stop to pick up produce, tons of cordwood, railroad ties, farm products, and livestock. Oldtimers recall hearing that, sometimes, so many large vessels were in the creek that one could walk shore to shore merely by stepping from one to another. This account seems feasible as a 1911 U.S. Engineers report indicates 372 steamers and 206 sailing vessels loaded there in one year. Little Ferry, established in 1748, was located on the Machodoc Creek near where the Route 218 bridge crosses the creek. George Washington mentions in his diary that he crossed the Machodoc at Little Ferry in 1763 and 1764. Little Ferry ceased operations in 1907.

When the Naval Proving Ground was established, many employees lived at Colonial Beach. Since a trip to the beach was shorter and quicker by water, it was not long before an enterprising man, Captain Bruce, began a morning and evening boat run between Dahlgren and Colonial Beach. According to Frederick

Dock, looking out over the river at Neill. Neill was located south of Gambo Creek at the Machodoc Creek. *Submitted by Delores Shea*

View of Machodoc Creek taken in 1960. *Virginia Department of Historic Resources, Richmond, Virginia*

Tilp in *That Was Potomac River*, there was a "milk ferry" in the 1920s and 1930s that ran morning and evening across the mouth of the Machodoc Creek between Baber's Point Dairy Farm and Dahlgren. It carried both passengers and dairy products.

Spy Hill, in the Tetotum area sitting 160 feet high, was named during the Revolutionary War because of its good viewing point to watch for English ships coming up the river. Charts of 1878 show this area as McMaria Bluff. Baber's Point was named for landowner Colonel Thomas B. Baber, who purchased the property from the Washington family in 1828. Charts of 1727 call it Ducking Stool Point; charts of 1862 call it Washington Point, and charts of 1926 call it Baber's Point.

— ROSIER'S CREEK —

Dividing part of King George County and Westmoreland County is Rosier's Creek, named for John Rosier, who patented land here in 1651. The emigrant John Washington built Washington Mill in 1662 at the headwaters of Rosier's Creek. At the head of tidewater was Millville and about one mile downstream was Weedon's Mill. Other mills on this creek were Watts Mill and Monroe Mill. Near the mouth was Rosier's Point, with one of the few tidemills on the river. There was another Washington Mill located on the Machodoc Creek where it narrows and passes through property near present-day Route 616.

— THE RAPPAHANNOCK RIVER —

The Rappahannock River, named for an Indian word meaning "alternating stream, the ebb and flow of a tidal river," for generations was used as a "road" from Fredericksburg and nearby areas to Washington, D.C., Alexandria, and to ports down the Chesapeake Bay. Many planters along the Rappahannock owned single-masted sloops. By the mid-1600s, sawmills were erected along the river by shipwrights and carpenters and boat building became important. In 1716, John Fontaine wrote in his journal, "a place called Taliaferro's Mount...from whence we had a fine view of the river which is navigable for large ships and has several fine islands." Records indicate that about eighty-five ships had entered the Rappahannock by 1769. Navigation on the river increased as a number of vessels came and went, including the *Planter* arriving at Port Royal laden with indentured servants in 1774. As early as 1828, there was regular schooner service to Baltimore and Norfolk. In 1846, the schooner *Mary* sailed from Port Conway laden with cargo. In the early 1900s, Weems steamboats stopped at thirty-two landings along the ninety-three-mile Rappahannock, many of them in King George. In 1907, the *Rappahannock River Line* traveled from Baltimore to several King George landings, including Wilmont, Greenlaw's Wharf, Port Conway, Hop Yard, and more.

In one of his newspaper columns, "Toot! Toot! Goodbye!," Thomas Lomax Hunter (1875–1948) wrote,

> *I was born on the shores of the Rappahannock River and the steamboats that bore me and my fathers back and forth, and up and down this river, played a high part in the life of the dwellers of the river valley...In the days just behind us the country merchant had his goods shipped from Baltimore or Fredericksburg to the nearest wharf on the Rappahannock or Potomac Rivers. Merchants kept a wagon and pair of horses to go to these wharves and bring the merchandise to the stores...that was yesterday.*

Small, but thriving, Port Conway was located near the present James Madison Memorial Bridge in King George across the river from the larger river town, Port Royal. In 1783, Francis Conway proposed to lay off lots for a town opposite Port Royal. Although the county court produced plans for a town in 1803, the plan did not materialize at that time, and the lots were sold off to individual owners. The Port Conway wharf reached out into deep water, where barrels were rolled onto ships. Later, pushcarts on rails were used. During the War Between the States, Union Army Engineers built a floating wharf for its gunboats. Port Conway continued as a town until well into the twentieth century.

Rappahannock ferries crisscrossed the river from King George landings to the opposite shore. As early as 1702, a ferry crossed at Woodlawn and in 1730, according to an article in a 1979 *Northern Neck of Virginia Historical Society Magazine*, there was a ferry that operated on the Rappahannock for eighty-five years near the Sealston area. This ferry operated under four successive owners: Anthony Seals, Joseph Berry, Thomas Casson, and Francis Conway II. Records of 1734 indicate there was a ferry at Millbank, the land of Samuel Skinker. Doniphan's ferry operated from 1755 to 1760. Ferries also crossed to the landings of John Moore and James Hackley, and another crossed between Taliaferro's Mount in Caroline County to Joseph Berry's land in King George County.

In the early 1800s, the steamboat era began with frequent runs from Fredericksburg, Alexandria, and Baltimore and continued for many years. The 176-foot *Potomac*, built in 1894, provided day trips with stops at several landings along the Rappahannock, including Greenlaw's Wharf, Nanzatico, Cleve, Hop Yard, and Wilmont Wharf. According to some, Hop Yard served a small community named for the hops grown among the vegetables of an adjoining farm where beer was brewed. Wilmont Wharf lay at the base of a cliff on the north bank of the Rappahannock. Bricks were made and shipped from the Wilmont area. Nearby are the remains of the Bristol Iron Works founded in 1721 by John Bristol.

James Madison Bridge. *Virginia Department of Historic Resources, Richmond, Virginia*

Greenlaw's Wharf was a small landing on the north bank. Upstream, the river forms a deep bend called Horsehead Turn. Another bend in the twisting river is known as Devil's Elbow. Other King George landmarks along the Rappahannock include Walsingham, Cleve, Belle Grove, Berry Plain, and Port Conway, where President James Madison was born.

In 1934, the first James Madison Memorial Bridge was constructed across the Rappahannock River. In 1940, the Potomac River Bridge opened and, in 1980, the new James Madison Memorial Bridge opened. The opening of these two bridges created new highways and opportunities for the people of King George County.

Harry Nice Bridge, previously called the Morgantown Bridge and the Potomac River Bridge, spans nearly two miles across the Potomac River.
Submitted by Carlton and Lois Griffin

The Virginia Department of Game and Inland Fisheries' Land's End Wildlife Management Area is situated along the north shore of the Rappahannock River near Nanzatico. This area boasts of a dense bald-eagle breeding population and a number of neotropical landbirds. These lands were once home to a sizable population of Nanzatico Indians, who farmed and fished along the Rappahannock shores for hundreds of years. This area is riddled with the remnants of their presence, including a number of burial mounds that have recently been identified.

The Woodlawn Historic and Archaeological District is an 899-acre historic, riverfront plantation located along the north bank of the Rappahannock River and the west bank of Gingoteague Creek.

Our surrounding waters are now mostly enjoyed by recreational boaters, and nearby scenic creeks provide excellent kayaking and canoeing. There are two public ramps for small boats and canoes—one at Wilmont on the Rappahannock and another at the three-acre Wayside Park located on the Potomac near the Harry W. Nice Bridge. Toby's Point, located at Wilmont, is part of the Rappahannock River Valley National Wildlife Refuge. Wayside Park is open year round and has a public beach and picnic areas. Another free public landing will soon open for King George County residents in the Hop Yard housing development. Barnesfield Park is located near Wayside Park on land that was once part of the Hooe family plantation. This 175-acre park has nature trails, picnic areas, a playground, and several ballfields.

King George waters are still used for some commercial ventures, and a few local watermen still eke out a living fishing and crabbing.

Barges and tugboats are seen on the Potomac almost daily. Recently, barges entered the Rappahannock River to deliver several nineteen-by-seventy-foot fermentation tanks to a landing near Farley Vale, where they were later delivered by truck to Elkton, Virginia, in the Shenandoah Valley.

The art of boat building is still practiced. Mr. Carlton Griffin builds his boat. *Submitted by Carlton and Lois Griffin*

Wilmont located on the southeastern tip of the county at Bristol Mines Run and the Rappahannock River. It is a public landing and has also been used over the years as a brick factory. *Painting by David Lee and owned by Kenneth and Elizabeth Lee*

The *Vivian Hannah* is a Mississippi paddlewheel ship privately owned by Stanley and Vivian Hannah Palivoda. It operates on Upper Machodoc Creek. It can accommodate more than 150 passengers with three floors of amenities, including many nautical antiques and an original English pub imported from England, reminiscent of the late 1800s on the Potomac River. There are no propellers like modern-day boats.

Map of King George County, 1859. *King George Courthouse*

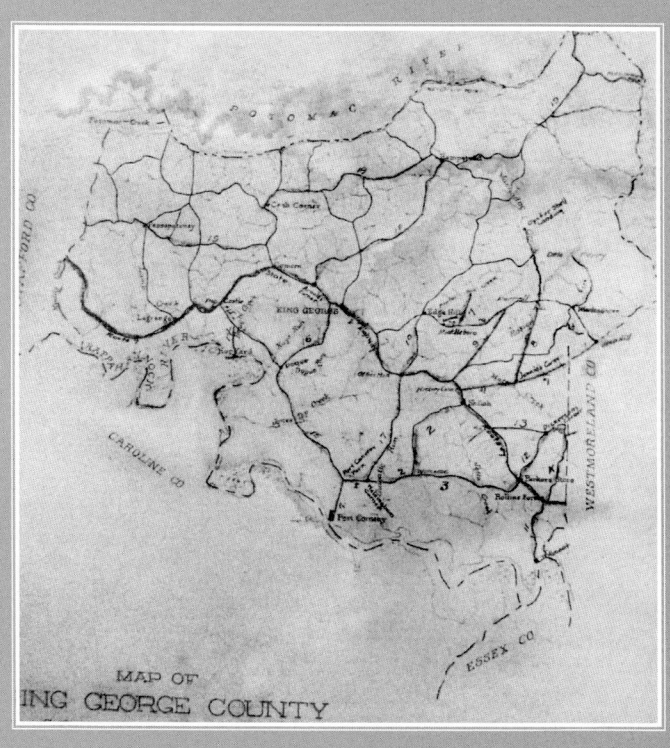

Map of King George County, 1917. Drawn by Jesse Newton, it depicts the road system prior to the Potomac River Bridge and the James Madison Bridge. *King George Courthouse*

Coors Beer planned to open a new brewery in McGayhesville, Virginia, in the Shenandoah Valley. These brewery drums were purchased from Germany and were loaded on barges for a journey up the Rappahannock River. At a location near Farley Vale, they are awaiting the long and tedious journey by truck over the mountains to Elkton, avoiding underpasses, low lights, and heavy traffic. In April 2006, the last of the drums left King George. *Photo by Elizabeth Lee*

Several families along the Potomac River were delighted when they spotted Jamestown's *Godspeed* replica sailing past. In August, after visiting several large ports along the East Coast, the *Godspeed* again passed King George as it sailed up the Potomac to Stafford County's Aquia Landing, completing its Four Hundredth Anniversary tour.

The appearance of a local businessman's eighty-four-foot sternwheeler, *Vivian Hannah*, on the Machodoc Creek recalls what life was like during King George County's yesteryears.

— Travel by Land —

Travel by road was the least likely option for a person wanting to get from one place to another. From earliest times, Native Americans traveled more by dugout than by making trails through the woods. When the English settlers came, there were no roads. Homes were built on or near access to water where goods could be brought in and shipped out. Those landowners whose property was not on the river bought access strips from their neighbor.

As the county became more populated, the county court would assign individuals to be "Keepers of the Road." Such individuals were responsible for

Horse and buggy, driven by Ida Green Moore, was a typical mode of transportation in the early 1900s. She is parked in front of an unidentified King George store. It is believed that this picture was taken about 1915. *Submitted by Jean Moore Graham*

maintenance to the portion of the road assigned to them. This position was taken seriously. Individuals could be fined heavily for failing to keep the road passable.

In 1884, a petition was filed, signed by sixty King George residents, asking "that a bridge be built across the stream called and known as Machodoc Run. This county road which leads from King George Court House to Hampstead is often impassable because of the precipitous ascent and descent, especially during the times of heavy rains." The petition continues, "that across this stream is the only way to the wharf on the Potomac River and St. Paul's Church…and now is a favorable time owing to the vicinity of a saw mill and consequent cheapness of materials." The bridge was to be completed by November 25, 1884, for the sum of $75.

Up into the twentieth century, roads were little more than wagon trails. Major roads through the King George County countryside were often impassable, especially at certain times of the year. In spring, many vehicles got stuck in quagmires resulting from melting snows and heavy rains. The expression "up to the hub" became a much-used colloquialism to illustrate this predicament. Washboard surfaces, made by placing logs side by side across the road, and potholes broke wagon wheels and axles and often caused coaches and carryalls to turn over.

When automobiles made their debut, few people thought much of them, and many could not afford to buy them. They broke down a lot and could not surmount hills like a strong team of horses. Harold Gouldman, in Dahlgren, wrote that it was impossible for an automobile to climb Pepper Mill hill in first gear. In 1900, there were only about 144 miles of paved roads in the entire United States, so one can only imagine how few, if any, there were in King George County. Within the last forty years, King George County still had county-maintained dirt roads.

On travel from Dahlgren in the early 1900s:

> *When people would start to town on the shopping trip, they would take at least four carrier pigeons with them. When they got stuck at Deep Bottom, they let a pigeon go on an air detail. We had to stand there and grab the bird as soon as it got back. When the message said "Deep Bottom," old Bob Pulliam would get one of these mules and ride out there, probably a half-hour trip. If the pigeons didn't come back in 25 minutes, they knew they'd gotten by Deep bottom. So the next place would be about 45 minutes to Peppermill Hill, and they would stand by to receive a pigeon. If no pigeon came back then, they would be on their way to Fredericksburg. It would be 5 or 6 hours before they had to be ready again.* McCollum, *Dahlgren,* 1977.

Research shows that in the United States in 1915, there were two horses for every three members of the farm population. Because of the greater distance that had to be traveled during day-to-day life, the residents in rural areas had more need for personal transportation than city dwellers. By 1929, there were more than five million autos and trucks on about six million farms.

With the opening of the James Madison Bridge in 1934 and the Potomac River Bridge in 1940, King George County was no longer isolated. In March 1941, Thomas Lomax Hunter quipped, "The bridge was her [Maryland's] baby and when it opened Virginia officialdom never noticed the event, and Maryland State police did duty on the Virginia side in handling the crowd. Today the roads leading to the bridge on both sides of the Potomac are tortuous and poorly made, but work is in progress to remedy this, and the route from the Potomac River Bridge to the James Madison Bridge will soon be virtually a straight line."

Williams Creek Bridge was built about 1941 as an easier access to the Dahlgren area and the base. This bridge has been replaced with the present bridge. *Submitted by Scott Tyndall*

Intersection of Highway 301 with Route 206, circa 1945, looking south. *Submitted by Francis Volante*

Intersection of Highway 301 with Route 206, today, looking north. *Photo by Jean Graham*

Prior to the opening of Interstate 95, Route 301 was a major north–south artery. With the opening of the Potomac River Bridge in 1940 and highway improvements in the 1950s, motels and restaurants flourished in King George County. This King George Motel is one of two from that era still being used as a motel. *King George County Museum*

By the early 1950s, the road connecting the two rivers had become a reality and a major highway leading north and south. With the improvements in the road system stimulated by the Eisenhower administration, motels and restaurants sprang up along the highway. At the same time, Colonial Beach was becoming the popular gambling attraction of the East Coast. By 1960, the traffic on the two-lane highway during a holiday weekend was stop and go. People could get out of their cars and walk faster than the car could move. The county's Board of Supervisors, concerned about this problem, moved for talks of widening the highway to a four-lane one. It was 1964 before this occurred. With the advent of a four-lane highway, the traffic circle at "the Circle" was destroyed. By the 1970s, two traffic lights on the highway became a reality. Today, ten traffic lights and an emergency light at the fire station control the flow of traffic in our county. At least two more lights are proposed.

The Potomac Grill, known as Wilkerson's Restaurant in Dahlgren, was a restaurant that flourished in the days before Interstate 95 was built. *King George County Museum*

— RAILROAD —

In about 1895, a railroad was planned to run east and west through the Northern Neck. The unknown reporter from Comorn wrote,

> *Our people are still very sanguine over what many consider a strong probability of a Northern Neck railroad. Businessmen from one end of the Neck to the other believe that a railroad through these counties would prove a potent factor in developing the whole country lying between the Potomac and Rappahannock into one of the finest sections of Virginia, for it is now an accepted fact that the Northern Neck possesses many natural advantages not to be found elsewhere. It is known that in addition to the resident capital, many thousands of northern capital await the construction of the proposed road, and will come here when the road is built, or even when its completion is guaranteed.*
>
> —Northern Neck, *Richmond Times*, April 28, 1895

This railroad never happened, and the counties in the Northern Neck, including King George, remained the rural area.

The Naval Proving Ground Railroad commenced operation in July 1942. The railroad track consisted of thirty miles of track along Pepper Mill Creek from Dahlgren to Fredericksburg. It carried supplies to the base, as well as passengers. The railroad was abandoned in 1957.

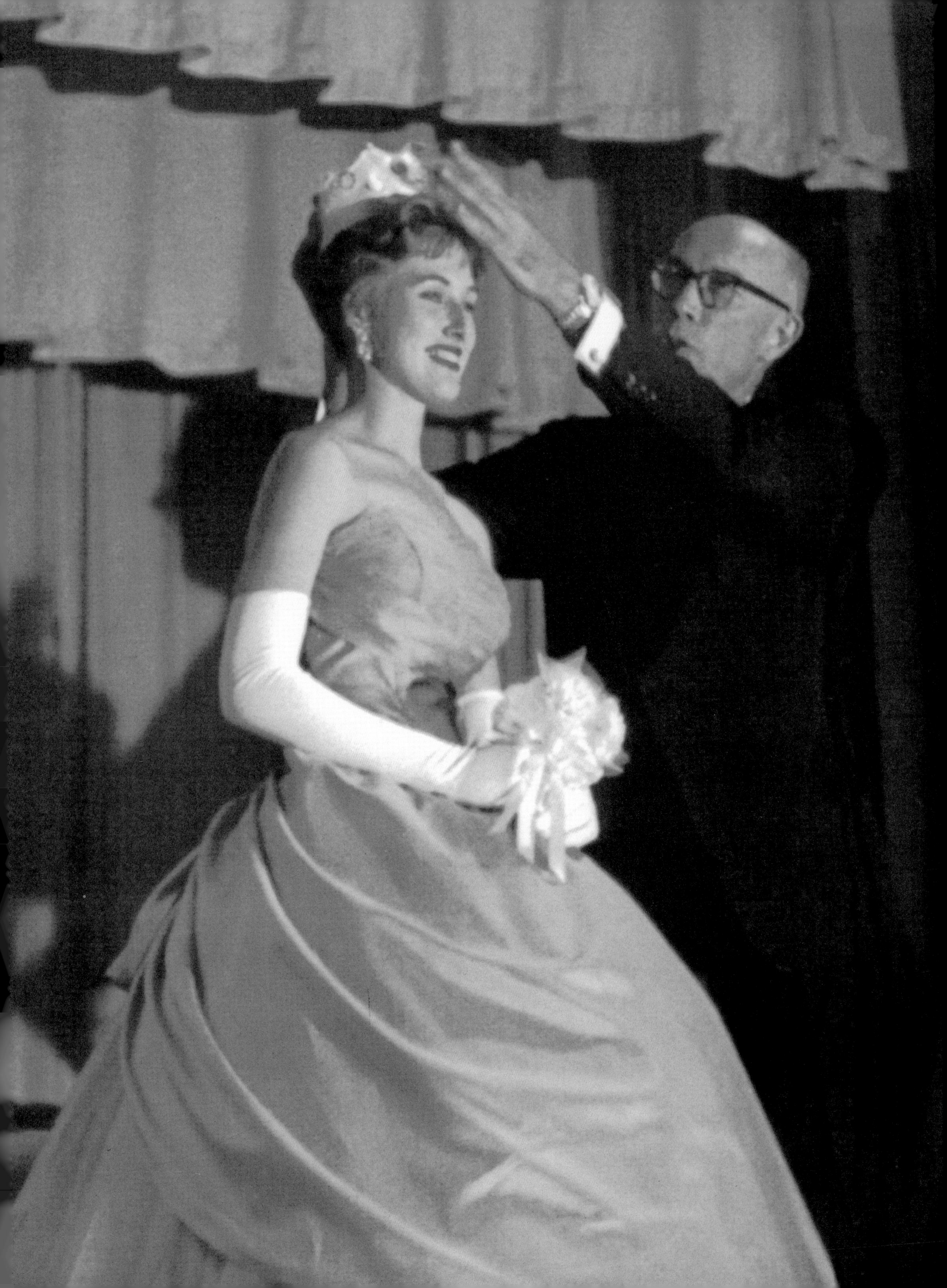

Chapter 10
Unforgettable Events

Although a rural community, King George County has offered many unforgettable times to its residents. In addition to events that shaped our country's history, the small events have shaped our community.

— Leedstown Resolutions —

Leedstown, now in Westmoreland County, was in King George County when on February 27, 1766, Thomas Ludwell Lee and Richard Henry Lee summoned 115 of their fellow patriots, forming the Westmoreland Association, and signed the Leedstown Resolutions, which had been drawn up at Chantilly, Westmoreland County, against the Stamp Act Tax. This was a declaration of independence, which antedated that which Jefferson was the author by more than ten years.

— King George County Fair —

Beginning in 1918, the county always had a fair called the "King George County Club and School Fair." Exhibits included everything from biscuits, canned pears, best bulls, cornstalks, written essays, drawings, and letter writing to knitting, embroidery, and tatting. The Sixth Annual Exhibition in 1923 was held on November 2, "if rainy, next day." The fairgrounds were located first beside the King George Motor Company building. Later, they were located behind the courthouse area.

Ribbons won by Maxfield Brown in the King George County Fair, 1925, 1927, and 1936. *King George County Museum*

— The James Madison Bridge Opening —

Prior to 1934, King George County was, for the most part, isolated from the north and south. Transportation to the north or south required use of a ferry or steamboat. On July 18, 1934, a ribbon-cutting ceremony was held for the newly constructed James Madison Bridge, connecting Port Conway to Port Royal. In attendance were Virginia Highway Commissioner Henry G. Shirley, Bishop Robert C. Jett, Senator Henry T. Wickham, Delegate T. Elliott Campbell, and Assistant Secretary of State R. Walton Moore. Miss Carol Blanton, daughter of Thomas H. Blanton, cut the ribbon. Thomas Lomax Hunter quoted the *Free Lance-Star* article in his Richmond news column "As It Appears to the Cavalier:" "Residents of the section are asked to bring their lunches, and to put in sufficient extra to take care in the aggregate of the many visitors expected."

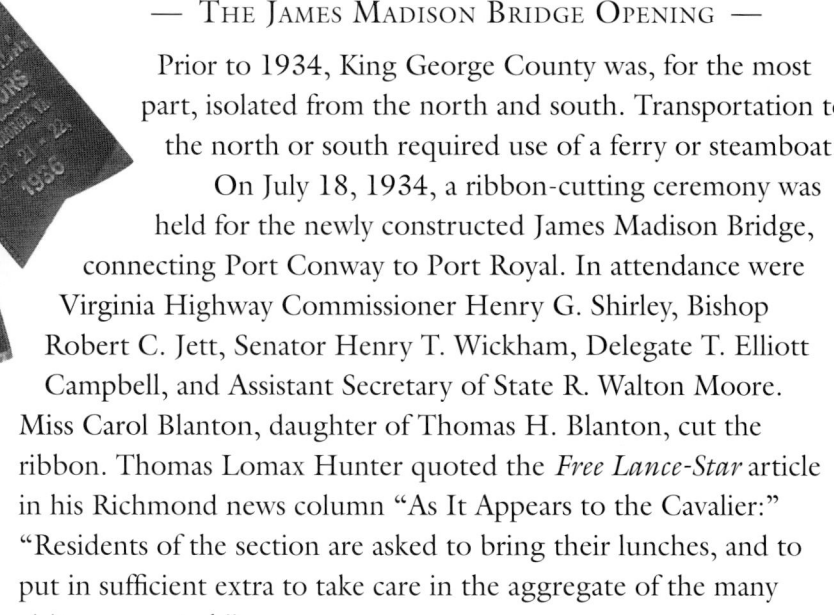

— The Morgantown Bridge Opening —

On December 14, 1940, the bridge linking Maryland and Virginia was opened. President Franklin D. Roosevelt attended the ceremonies. Maryland Governor Herbert R. O'Conor and State Road Commissioner Major Ezra Whitman attended also. Governor O'Conor cut the ribbon and spoke:

> *TODAY in these ceremonies marking the opening to traffic of this splendid new structure that will bind Maryland and Virginia closer than ever in ties of friendship, we see exemplification of the old truth that history moves in cycles. As we contemplate with unbounded satisfaction the completion of this modern aid to transportation, it is significant to recall that it was at Ludlow's Ferry, close by the Maryland end of the bridge, that the first ferry established in early*

The James Madison Bridge. *Virginia Department of Historical Resources, Richmond, Virginia*

colonial days constituted one of the first links in the North–South seaboard road connecting the colonies. This ferry was used by George Washington and the Revolutionary troops, and helped to expedite the transportation of soldiers to Yorktown, preceding the surrender of Cornwallis. I believe I am expressing the feelings of everyone present in voicing the hope that there will never be the occasion to make use of this new bridge across the Potomac to rush troops for the defense of our Country. Many rivers and streams in our Country have greater length and greater present-day use than the Potomac, but few of them are richer in background of association with the development of this Country during the pioneer days. In all the 300 or more years that Marylanders have crossed and recrossed the river to our sister-state of Virginia, there has never been a bridge of any sort from the river's mouth to the City of Washington, a distance of nearly one hundred miles. Certainly, therefore, today will go down in the history of these two great states as a truly memorable day. This bridge will be the only one crossing on the Potomac River between the District of Columbia and the mouth of the river at the Chesapeake Bay and will provide access and uninterrupted communication between the two states now separated by the river. It will provide an alternate route for tourists traveling from Baltimore and the North to Richmond, Norfolk, and the South. It will provide easier and cheaper access for marketing of produce in the section of Virginia known as the Northern Neck and points South to the Markets of Washington, Baltimore, and

President Franklin D. Roosevelt, present at the opening ceremonies for the Potomac River Bridge, December 14, 1940. *Maryland Transportation Authority*

the North. It will connect Baltimore, Washington, and the North with the historic points of Virginia, such as Williamsburg, Yorktown, Jamestown, Wakefield, and Stratford by a shorter route than the existing route via Fredericksburg. It will constitute an important link in the Nation's North–South Coastal highway, with easy, grades and straight alignment from New England to Florida. The economic and social values of this bridge are at once apparent. The advantages to the people of the adjacent Maryland and Virginia counties in expediting the natural interchange of social and commercial relations are easily realized, and since the advent of the automobile, the need for a physical connection of the highways has become pressing. Prior to the advent of the automobile, the river itself formed the connection by furnishing means for transportation by boat, but since the advent of the automobile, transportation by boat is considered too slow as compared with the speed of motor traffic. The idea of constructing a bridge across the Potomac has been agitated for fifteen years or more, but the first active participation of our State was in 1932, when the State Roads Commission came into the picture with a report relating to a proposed bridge across the Potomac. After much consideration by various agencies, the Federal Emergency Administration of Public Works tendered to the State Roads Commission of Maryland a grant offer in the amount of 45%, totaling $1,766,900. This grant later was increased to $2,351,970, as against the total cost of $5,226,000. This was somewhat in excess of the original estimate, which was raised by several developments, chief among them, the requirements of the War Department that the main channel span be shifted to the eastward, thus increasing this span from 650 feet to 800 feet. The length of the bridge, including the Maryland approach is, 11,477 feet, and its clear height above the water at the main channel span is 135 feet. The engineering difficulties encountered and overcome made construction of this bridge one of the engineering feats of the past decade.

To add more excitement to the opening of the bridge, two young men, Roland "Blue" Burgess and Walter Mason, set off from Dahlgren to Fredericksburg in a J-3 Piper Cub hoping to pick up a part for Mason's car. They spotted the crowd of people below. Burgess decided to make a pass under the new bridge at its highest point. After his successful run, Mason, who was just learning to fly, made a second pass. On to Fredericksburg they flew, landing at Shannon Airport, leaving a crowd of astonished onlookers.

Today, the bridge is referred to as the Potomac River Bridge, or the Harry W. Nice Bridge.

— Gambling on the Potomac —

In the early 1950s, gambling and slot machines were legal in Maryland. Since the Maryland line was at the low water mark of the Virginia shore, gambling establishments were built out on the water with access to King George and Westmoreland residents. Colonial Beach was famous for its Reno and Monte Carlo piers, being dubbed "the Las Vegas on the Potomac." King George had piers at Fairview Beach and Belvedere Beach. Once a person stepped onto the pier, they were no longer in Virginia and were subject to Maryland laws. Barroom brawls sent the perpetrators on a boat ride to Maryland and a Maryland jail.

Consequently, Belvedere Beach became an entertainment center, introducing popular entertainers, including singer Patsy Cline.

Belvedere Beach. Besides the gambling, Belvedere Beach was known for its live entertainment in its grand ballroom.
King George County Museum

Chapter 10: Unforgettable Events

— FALL FESTIVAL —

In 1959, the first Fall Festival was held in King George County. The festival was organized as a community service, bringing participating organizations together in closer understanding and cooperation, and as a means of assisting the Rescue Squad and fire departments in fundraising. It has been the longest continual festival in the county. Some of the themes depicted over the years were "Three Cheers for the Red, White, and Blue," "Say It With Music," and "King George—We're the Best."

Top left: The 1963 Fall Festival float entry by the Farm Bureau of King George County depicts a rosy future for farming and livestock in King George. *King George County Museum*

Top right: The King George High School Band performs in one of the earlier Fall Festivals. *John Hunter Collection, King George County Museum*

Bottom left: Members of the King George County Historical Society walk in the 2003 Fall Festival parade. Left to right: Georgia Bussink, Valerie Hill, Gena Bussink and son Graham, Ginger Hill, Andrew Brown, Doris Gouldman, Bobbe King, and Jean Graham. *Submitted by Elizabeth Lee*

Bottom right: Members of the King George County Historical Society walk in the 2002 Fall Festival parade. Left to right: Walter Gallahan, Karen Schouweiler, Andrew Brown, Betty Lou Braden, Koontz Campbell, Elizabeth Lee, and Jake Schouweiler. *Submitted by Elizabeth Lee*

Beverley Clare waves at the camera in the 1960 Fall Festival. She is representing the Circle Supermarket. Driving the car is Clifford Hudson. In the background is Clift Ford Motor Company. *King George County Museum*

State Senator Paul Mann crowns Ann Richardson. Ann was the first queen of the Fall Festival, 1959. *Submitted by Ann Richardson Gautier*

Mrs. Lucy Grymes of Marmion stands in front of this 1961 model of Marmion, which was entered in the Fall Festival Parade. *King George County Museum*

The Lions Club Talent Show coincided with the Fall Festival. In this 1962 photo, Morton Jones, Ernest Combs, and Dwight Storke play and sing for the audience. *King George County Museum*

The 1961 Fall Festival queen, Linda Berry, is crowned by the 1960 queen, Judy Griffith. *King George County Museum*

Chapter 10: Unforgettable Events 167

— THE FIRE OF 1963 —

    The March winds and dry season of 1963 were ripe for a fire. Several fires had already hit the county hard. Seventy-nine acres had burned in Dogue in March. In April, a resident who lived near Route 301 was burning trash when the wind caught it and carried it outside the container. The fire quickly spread from the west side of Highway 301, across the dugout portion of the southbound two lanes of 301 under construction, and across the two-lane highway. From there, it traveled eastward into Westmoreland County before it was put under control by a backfire at Maple Grove. At least sixteen fire companies from as far as Kilmarnock, White Stone, and Culpeper responded to the fire. Men from Fort Belvoir and A.

The Bicentennial Wagon Train came through King George in early June 1976. It parked in Strother's field, on Route 301, and was well attended by county residents. *Submitted by Mary Jean Inscoe*

168   *King George County: A Pictorial History*

P. Hill and a helicopter from Quantico also helped in the efforts to contain the fire. The town of Colonial Beach was on alert to evacuate. Three homes were destroyed in King George County, two of them vacant. Countless homes were saved.

— BICENTENNIAL WAGON TRAIN STOP —

In 1975, as the Bicentennial of the American Revolution neared, people began planning a multitude of events to mark the occasion. One such event was the Bicentennial Wagon Train Pilgrimage. The plan, a nationwide bicentennial event lasting more than a year, was to have authentically reproduced covered wagons travel along the well-known trails of their ancestors and converge at the Valley Forge National Historic Park to celebrate on July 4, 1976. Pennsylvania bought and gave a wagon to each state to use as the official state wagon and underwrote the project. Private wagons were welcomed to join. Some people took their children out of school for the whole year to travel with the train. Each train had a musical show that performed for local communities and then embarked from each state to their final destination. Scrolls were carried from town to town by the wagons, where residents could sign vowing "to commemorate this nation's Bicentennial, we hereby dedicate ourselves anew to the precepts of our founding fathers: …We hold these truths to be self evident, that all men are created equal, that they are endowed by their Creator with certain unalienable Rights, that among these are Life, Liberty, and the pursuit of Happiness."

In June 1976, the Virginia Wagon Train stopped in King George County in Ashby Strother's field off of Route 301. As with many of the bicentennial events, residents came dressed in their finest eighteenth-century frocks made especially for the celebration.

Top: Boating has been a recreation dear to the hearts of King George citizens from early times. *Submitted by Carlton and Lois Griffin*

Bottom: Youngsters enjoy the sunshine and a dip in the Potomac River. *Submitted by Carlton and Lois Griffin*

— TODAY —

Events that are now becoming a regular part of our county's history are the Home Show in March and the Relay for Life in May.

From the open-air movie theater at Arnold's Corner, hanging out at Tommy's Snack Bar, the Friday-night Subteen Club dances at the firehouse, or roller skating at Fairview Beach, the county has never lacked activities for those who could drive to get to them. Being a county on two rivers, swimming and boating have also been recreational activities enjoyed throughout our history. Other recreational activities have included polo games at Powhatan and fox hunting.

Chapter 10: Unforgettable Events 169

Bibliography

Beitzel, Edwin W. *Life On the Potomac River.* Washington, DC: Kirby Lithograph Company, 1968.

Bushnell, David I., Jr. *Indian Sites Below the Falls of the Rappahannock, Virginia.* Washington, DC: Smithsonian Institution, 1937.

Davis, Jackson. Papers. Neg. 0588, MSS 3072. Special Collections. University of Virginia Library.

Flemer, Carl F., Jr. *Four Centuries of Little Known Washington Parish History.* Richmond, VA: Lewis Printing Company, 1991.

Gutheim, Frederick. *The Potomac.* New York: Grosset and Dunlap Publishers, 1968.

Hening, William Waller. *The Statutes at Large: Being A Collection of All the Laws of Virginia, From the First Session of the Legislature, in the Year 1619.* Richmond, VA: 1821. Facts from assorted volumes.

Holly, David C. *Tidewater By Steamboat.* Baltimore, MD: Johns Hopkins University Press, 1991.

Krick, Robert K. *9th Virginia Cavalry.* Lynchburg, VA: H. E. Howard, 1982.

"A Long Life, A Good Life on the Potomac." *National Geographic*, October 1976.

McCollum, Kenneth G., ed. *Dahlgren.* Dahlgren, VA: Naval Surface Weapons Center, 1977.

McCutcheon, Marc. *The Writer's Guide to Everyday Life in the 1800s.* Cincinnati, OH: Writer's Digest Books, 1993.

Netherton, Nan, et al. *In the Path of History: Virginia Between the Rappahannock and the Potomac: An Historical Portrait.* Falls Church, VA: Higher Education Publications, Inc., 1999.

Northern Neck Historical Magazine. Selected articles from various issues.

Payne, James N. "Early Days of Dahlgren and Before." *Northern Neck of Virginia Historical Magazine*, December 1990.

Shackelford, George Green. "Nanzatico, King George County, Virginia." *Virginia Magazine of History and Biography*, October 1965.

Stuart, Hugh Roy. "Selected Stories About King George County and Surrounding Areas." Unpublished paper, 1962.

Swanton, John Reed. *The Indian Tribes of North America.* Washington, DC: Smithsonian Institution, 1953.

Tilp, Frederick. *This Was Potomac River.* Alexandria, VA: Self-published, 1978.

U.S. Bureau of the Census. U.S. Census Records. 1860 and 1870.

Wilstach, Paul. *Potomac Landings.* Indianapolis, IN: Bobbs-Merrill Company, 1920.

Selected reports from the history files of King George County Museum & Research Center.

Selected newspaper articles from out-of-print newspapers.

Index

A
Acors, Nellie, 58
Acowehtank, 144
Agar, Edward, 68
Ager, E., 72
Albion, 105, 146
Alexander family, 85, 143
Alford, G., 60
Algernon, William, 91
Allen, J., 72
Allen, William J., 75
Allensworth, Bobby, 136
Allensworth, J., 72
Allensworth, Louise, 128
Allensworth, Susanne, 132
Allensworth, Webster, 29
Allison, Ethel, 58
Alto, 104
Ambar School, 127, 128
Anacostia (steamer), 145
Antioch Baptist Church, 115, 116
Applegarth, George, 147
Arcadia, 104
Armstrong, Doyle Emerson, 77
Armstrong, E., 60
Armstrong, James, 67
Armstrong, William, 67
Arnold, James A., 57, 146
Arnold, James, 87
Arnold, John, 107
Arnold, Sgt. M. B., 72
Arnold, Mary Frances, 116
Arnold, Napoleon B., 68
Arnold, Lt. P. M., 72
Arnold, Thomas Thornton, 68, 107
Ashland, 103
Ashton, Charles H., 23
Ashton, Dade, 91
Ashton, George Dent, 93
Ashton, Henry Alexander, 93
Ashton, John, 93
Ashton, Lewis, 91
Ashton, Col. Peter, 82
Ashton, Sonny, 28, 136
Ashton, Stuart, 40
Aspen Grove, 40
Atkins, Cdr. C. T., 60
Atkins, N., 60
Atwell, H., 72
Ayers, Joe, 58

B
Baber, Lt. D. L., 72
Baber, Thomas B. B., 68, 93, 116, 149
Baber's Mill, 50
Baber's Point Dairy Farm, 149
Bacon's Rebellion, 14
Bailey, James, 68
Baily, R., 71
Baird, M., 60
Baker, J., 72
Baker, James, 67
Baker, John, 96
Baker, Shirley, 132
Baker House, 103
Bandy, W., 60
Bankhead, William, 41
Bank of King George, 65
Barker, A., 72
Barker, G., 72
Barker, Katherine, 58
Barnes, Frank, 146
Barnes, Thomas, 147
Barnesfield, 72, 105, 145, 147
Barnesfield Dairy, 52
Barnesfield Park, 31, 152
Bass, Jeff, 63
Bayliss, Davis, 23
Bay, Mrs., 58
Bayne, Lilla, 57
Bayne, Patterson, 57
Bedford, 105, 108
Bedford Landing, 143
Beitzel's, 145
Belle Grove, 34, 97, 98, 152
Bellomy, J., 60
Belvedere Beach, 165
Berkeley, Gov. Sir William, 14
Bernard family, 97
Berry, John, 57
Berry, Joseph, 99, 151
Berry, Lawrence, 100
Berry, Mr., 114
Berry, William, 99
Berry Plain, 99, 100, 152
Berthaville, 61
Bevan, Thomas H., 23
Bicentennial Wagon Train Pilgrimage, 169
Billingsley, Joseph A., Sr., 64
Billingsley, Joseph F., 70
Billingsley, Lewis J., 23
Bill of Rights, 38
Birchwood Power Plant, 64
Blake, Dave, 28
Blanton, Carol, 162
Blanton, Thomas H., 162
Bleak Hill, 103
Bloomsbury, 105
"Boomtown," 58
Booth, John Wilkes, 43, 74, 89, 90–91
Boundary Changes, 18
Bowen, Stephen P., 125
Bowie, P., 71-72
Bowie, T., 72

Bowler, Blanche, 128
Bowler, Eva, 128
Bowler, Tommy, 128
Boyd's Hole, 73, 85, 144, 147
Bradshaw, Joan, 132
Brannican, Lawrence, 142
Brent, A., 60
Brick House Landing, 148
Brissey, John, 68
Bristol, John, 151
Bristol Iron Works, 48, 151
Bristol Mines Run, 153
Britton, Matthew, 22
Brooks, Cedell, Jr., 22
Brooks, Louise Nuckols, 106
Brown, Belle, 93
Brown, E., 60
Brown, Mac, 58
Brown, Mr., 114
Brown, Solomon J. S., 25, 68, 109
Brown, W. W., 23
Brown, William S., 23, 25, 40, 68, 70, 93, 108, 125
Brown, William W., 25
Bruce, Capt., 148
Bruce, Robert F., 68
Brunswick Parish, 111
Buchanan, Lt. Cdr. C., 60
Buena Vista, 105, 92, 106
Burgess, Ronald "Blue," 165
Burnett, James W., 68
Burnley, 104
Burns, Jim, 136
Burnsides, Ambrose, 103
Burrell, Ernest, 114
Burrell, Fred, 58

C
C. E. Davis tomato cannery, 147
Caledon, 85, 86, 144
Caledon Natural Area, 144
Calvert, Cecil, 15
Cameron, 105
Cameron, Larry, 137
Cameron, Mary Ann Clift, 135
Campbell, Archibald, 112
Campbell, Delegate T. Elliot, 162
Canning, 21, 22, 106, 109
Capital City, 144
Carlo pier, 165
Carter, Charles, 21, 77, 99
Carter, John, 99
Carter, Landon, 93, 99
Carter, Robert, 15
Carter, Robert "King," 99
Caruthers, Franklin Clark, 76
Caruthers, Dr. Viola, 105
Carver, John, 68, 69
Carver, Lovell, 68

Carver, Cpl. R. E., 72
Carver, R. T., 71
Casson, Thomas, 151
Cedar Grove, 87, 89, 144
Celtwood, 100
Charles I, 15
Charles II, 15
Charles H. Harris's Store, 65
Chatterton, 82, 83
Chatterton's Landing, 143
Cheatham, Mr., 58
Cherry Green, 102
Cherry Point, 100
Chin, H., 60
Chin, Robert H., 77
Chingoteague Creek, 13
Chinn, Jesse, 127
Chotank, 94
Chotank Creek Natural Area Preserve, 144
Circle Inn, 56
Circle Market, 57
"Circle, the", 159
Circle, The, 56
Clare, Beverley, 167
Clare, L. V., 56, 57
Clare, Logan, 27
Clare, Veola, 107
Clare, W. W., 57, 60
Clarence, 90
Clark, Wayne, 136
Clarke, G., 60
Clarke, Wayland, 40
Cleek, W., 60
Cleve, 99, 151, 152
Cleve Packing Plant, 64
Cleveland, 106
Cleves, Alvan B., 72
Cleydael, 43, 89, 90, 91, 123
Clift, Earl Thomas, 128
Clift, Gene, 27, 28
Clift, James M., 128
Clift, Leah Ann Allen, 53
Clift, Margaret Harris, 56
Clift, Matt, 53
Clift, Mrs., 58
Clift, Robert F., 128
Clift, Sigsbee, 27
Clift, Vashti Harris, 135
Clift Motor Company, 27
Clift's Garage, 63
Cloud, Phillip, 132
Clovis Point, 14
Coakley, A., 72
Coakley, Daniel, 93, 125
Coakley, Daniel W., 23
Coakley, Wayland, 40
Coates, Tommy, 136
Coates, Walter, 114

171

Coghill, Roy, 58
Collins, Capt. C. R., 72
Colonial Beach, 144, 148
Colton, William, 125
Columbian (steamboat), 142
Combs, Ernest, 167
Combs, Mamie, 128
Comorn, 159
Comorn House, 95
Conway, Francis, 36, 67, 150
Conway, Francis, II, 151
Cook, Eva, 128
Cottage Wharf, 143
county seal, 25
Courthouse Market, 55
Cox, John, 67
Crismond, H. W., 72
Crismond, L. E., 72
Crismond, Mable McGinniss, 128
Cromwell's, Oliver, 15
Crosses, 127
Crowley, H., 60
Culpeper, Lord, 15
Cushing, Wayne, 136
Cuttatawomen, 12

D
Dade, Ashton G., 69
Dade, F. L., 72
Dade, Fannie B., 74
Dade, Frank L., 69
Dade, Langhorne, 87
Dade, Lucia, 74
Dade, Lucien, 74, 104
Dade, Townsend, Sr., 144
Dade family, 103, 105, 143
Daffen, J., 60
Dahlgren, 57, 129, 148, 149, 157
Dahlgren, John Adolphus, 57
Dahlgren Rescue Squad, 28
Dahlgren United Methodist, 123
Dahlgren United Methodists, 122
Davies, Fred, 65
Davies, G. W., 72
Davis, Gusty, 23
Davis, I., 60
Davis, Jessie, 58
Dawson, Mary Waugh, 37
Dawson, Robert, 58
Dawson, Russell, 58
DeAtley, Miss Thelma, 132
Dent, George, 147
Deputy, David, 19
DeShazo, Raleigh, 28
DeShazo's store, 55
Dickens, Sgt. J., 72
Dickens, John R., 70
Dickerson, Elsie, 128
Dickerson, Ethel, 128
Dickerson, Harold, 128
Dickerson, James, 128
Dickerson, Louise, 128
Dickinson, John, 100
Dickinson, John F., 68
Dickinson, William H., 68
Dido Wharf, 147
Didonato, A. R., 28
Dillard, James, 69
Dinwiddie, John, 21, 22
Dishman, R., 71
Dishman, Sam, 42
Dissington, 105
Dobson, Clarence "Moose," 22
Dodd, George, 114

Dodd, Kenneth, 114
Dodson, Archie, 58
Doeg tribe, 13
Dogue, 127
Dogue House, 10
Doherty, Marie, 40, 108
Doniphan's ferry, 151
Doris, 132
Dougherty, Margaret, 99
Ducking Stool Point, 149
dugout, 17
Dunlop, John, 116, 119
Dunmore, Lord, 36
Dunn, Eddie, 132

E
Eagle's Nest, 83, 142
Earle, Rear Admiral Ralph, 57
Ebenezer Baptist Church, 114, 116
Eden, 105
Edgehill, 102, 127
Edgehill Post Office, 63
Edwards, James, 96
Edwards, P., 72
Edwards, T. J., 72
Ellerslie, 105
Elliott, G. B., 60
Elliott, Grayson, 60
Ellis, James, 68
Emmanuel Church, 113, 114
Emmaus, 103

F
Fairfax, Ferdinando, 125
Fairview Beach, 143, 144
Fairview School House, 116
Faith and Hope Society, 57
Fall Festival, 25, 166
Farley Vale, 104, 152
Farrell, Joseph V., 77
Faulkner, John E., 147
Feather, Jackie, 136
Fenwick, Bill, 26
Ferrell Chapel, 121
Ferrell, Jimmy, 132
Ferrell, John, 68
Ferrell, Nelson, 58
Ferrell, William Edward, 76, 77
Filmore, Daniel, 58
Firedland, 94
fire of 1963, 168
First Baptist Ambar, 119, 120, 122
Fisher, Lt., 58
Fitzhugh family, 80, 143
Fitzhugh, Alice Thornton, 100
Fitzhugh, D. M., 72
Fitzhugh, Daniel, 68
Fitzhugh, Daniel McCarty, 100
Fitzhugh, Elizabeth, 83
Fitzhugh, Lt. H. M., 72
Fitzhugh, Henry, 105
Fitzhugh, John, 100
Fitzhugh, John B., 147
Fitzhugh, Landon, 83
Fitzhugh, Louise, 58
Fitzhugh, Marcellus, 65, 72, 76
Fitzhugh, Robert, 68
Fitzhugh, Virginia Elizabeth, 128
Fitzhugh, William, 15, 36, 83, 84
Fitzhugh's Mill, 51
Fletcher's Chapel, 122
Foote, Sarah, 87
Foster, Capt. H. L., 72
Fowke family, 143

Fowkes Landing, 142
Frank, J., 72
Friedland, 73, 105
Friendly Cottage, 29, 80
Fritter, L. M., 60

G
Gaines, William H., 68
Gainey, Zachariah, 116
Gamble, Alexander, 147
Gambo Creek, 147
Garland, Griffin, 19
Garland, Max, 28
Garner, George, 60
Garner, W. R., 26
Garner, Willard, 55
Garnett, Emma, 93
Garnett, Henry Thomas, 93
Garnett's Mill, 50
Gattrell, Ester, 58
Gayle, Thomas Benton, III, 40, 127, 133, 135
Gemmell, G. P., 27
George II, 15
Gera, 127
Gibson, Jonathan, 21
Gingoteague Creek, 152
Glancey, John, 136
"Glebe Hanover," 41
Goby, 127
Godspeed (ship), 155
Golden, Glen Rollins, 128
Good Hope Baptist Church, 41, 116, 117
Gordon, Thomas, 67
Gorman, W. R., 26
Gouldman, Alexander B., 102
Gouldman, Annie, 128
Gouldman, Carlin, 128
Gouldman, J., 72
Gouldman, Lavalette, 128
Gouldman, Rouzie, 128
Graham, George Mason, 89
Grantswood, 73, 105
Gray, Cleveland, 58
Gray, Doug, 26
Gray, Douglas T., III, 77
Gray, Richard, 58
Green, Ernest "Capt. Billy," 140
Green, H., 60
Green Heights, 95
Green Heights School, 129
Green Hill, 108
Greenlaw, Joseph S., 68
Greenlaw, Thomas P., 70
Greenlaw's Wharf, 13, 49, 150, 151, 152
Griffin, Carlton, 153
Griffin, H., 71
Griffin, J., 71
Griffin, Mr., 58
Griffin, William H., 68
Griffith, Judy, 167
Grigsby, Caldwell A., 75
Grigsby, Cleveland, 42
Grigsby, George W., 74
Grigsby, William, 105
Grymes, George, 63
Grymes, Benjamin, 83, 147
Grymes, Mrs. Benjamin, 147
Grymes, Benjamin C., 57
Grymes, George E., 68
Grymes, George Edmund, 107
Grymes, George Nicholas, 107

Grymes, Lucy, 167
Grymes, Mr., 146
Grymes, Thomas J., 68
Grzeika, Joseph W., 22
Guest, Raymond, 101

H
Haar, Ltjg., 58
Hackley, James, 151
Hagley, 105
Hall, George, 46
Hall, J. B., 137
Hall, R., 72
Hamilton, William, 147
Hampstead, 156
Hanover Baptist Church, 114
Hanover Parish House, 113
Hanover Parish, 111, 112
Harnly, Lt. H. S., 60
Harris, Annie King, 55
Harris, Buddy, 114
Harris, Mamie Fitzhugh, 135
Harris, Dr. Roger, 42
Harris, Stephen F., 68
Harris, Thomas B., 55
Harrison, Emma, 58
Harrison, Philip T., 77
Harry Randall, 144
Harry W. Nice Bridge, 147, 152, 165
Hart, Billy, 136
Hart, John, 68
Harwood, Mary, 135
Hatcher, Hezekiah M., 77
Haynie, Mrs., 58
Hedrick Capt. D. I., 60
Heflin, W. N., 23
Heim, Elbert Stewart, 77
Henderson, Asbury, 23
Henderson, Charles, 68
Henderson, F., 72
Henderson, George S., 77
Henderson, Herbert, 69
Henderson, J. J., 71
Henderson, James, 69
Henderson, Leonard M., 77
Henderson, M., 60
Henderson, Martha Henson, 62
Henderson, William W., 142
Henry, Patrick, 147
Herbert, Harry T., 77
Herold, David, 91
Hobson, 90, 91
Hodge, Teddy, 132
Hoffman, Cdr. H. D., 60
Hoge, Caroline (Owens), 63
Hoge, Gertrude, 63
Hoge, Granville, 63
Hoge, James L., 63
Hoge, Jim, 61
Hoge, Willard, 63
Holbert, Richard, 68
Holbert, Richard H., 69
Holland, George S., 147
Hooe, 152
Hooe, Dr. A. B., 145
Hooe, Alexander Seymour, 94
Hooe, Mary Barnes, 91
Hooe, R. E., 71
Hooe, Seymour, 67, 68
Hooe family, 105
Hooe's Post Office, 61
Hooker, George Kelly, 77
Hop Yard, 145, 150, 151, 152

Hopyard Farm Dairy, 52
Howard, James B., 22
Howard's View Church, 121
Howard's View Mission, 119
Howland, H. H., 72
Howland, Harrison G., 128
Howland, Mary Virginia, 132
Howland, Niven, 114
Hudson, Estes, 76
Hudson, Frank T., 26
Hudson, Frank, 63
Hudson, J. D., 27
Hudson, Cpl. P., 72
Hudson, Pearl Clift, 128
Hudson, R. H., 68
Hudson, William T., 63
Hudson, William Warner, 73
Hudson-Morris Lodge No. 80, 30, 31
Huff, Caroline, 58
Hughes, Ron, 136
Humphries, Loch W., 147
Hunter, Edward J., 25
Hunter, F. C. S., 68
Hunter, Frederick C. S., 25
Hunter, Frederick Campbell Stuart, 39
Hunter, R. W., 108
Hunter, Surg. T. L., 72
Hunter, Thomas Lomax, 39, 40, 108, 150, 157, 162
Hunter Amphitheater, 135
Hylton, 34, 88

I
Igo, 54
Index Store, 54
Index, 127
Indian Town House, 15, 84, 85
Inscoe, Harry, Sr., 114
Inscoe, Minnie Pitts, 128
Inscoe, Welford, 132
Inscoe, William, 68
I-Opassus, 12

J
Jackson, Edmond, 116
Jackson, Thomas, 68
James, James J., 147
James A. Ferrell Store and Post Office, 62
James Madison Memorial Bridge, 54, 150, 152, 157, 162
Jane Moseley (sidewheeler), 144
Japasaw, 12
Jay, John W. R., 69
Jenkins, H. S., 60
Jenkins, J., 60
Jenkins, W. F., 60
Jenkins, William Clifton, 77
Jennings, Ed, 58
Jeter Lumberyard, 64
Jett, Columbia, 105
Jett, P. M., 69
Jett, Bishop Robert Cater, 105, 162
Jett, Dr. William Newton, 73, 105
Jewel, Tommy, 26
John King Company, 48
John W. Thompson (steamer), 144
Johnson, Beanoil, 75
Johnson, Collins, 26
Johnson, Donald M., 77
Johnson, Joseph, 42, 57, 75
Johnson, King David, 57

Johnson, Sonny, 26, 136
Johnson, Willie, 58
Jones Pond, 145
Jones, Basil, 69
Jones, Charles G., 70
Jones, Cpl. E., 72
Jones, Elizabeth, 41
Jones, J., 72
Jones, Sgt. J., 72
Jones, James, 35, 68, 72
Jones, James E., 68
Jones, Joseph, 36, 41, 68, 104
Jones, L., 72
Jones, Lewis, 69
Jones, Morton, 167
Jones, S., 72
Jones, Stanfield, 69
Jones, T. B., 23
Jones, W., 72
Jones, William, 68, 69

K
Kappa, Chief Gunner, 60
Kaufmann, Ray, 28
Kendall, Samuel, 68
Kennedy, Y., 72
Kerahocaks, 13
Kester, Paul, 103
King, Cynthia, 132
King, James Bagley, 23
King, John, 48
King, Virginia McGinniss, 128
King, William F., 68
King George I, 15
King George Cannery, 49
King George Elementary School, 129
King George Farmers Cooperative, 49
King George High School, 130, 134
King George Lodge No. 314, 31
King George Middle School, 135
King George Motor Company, 64
King George seal, 26
King George Volunteer Fire Association, 26
Kings Mill, 51
Krentel, Lt. P. A., 60
Kyle, Buster, 26
Kyle, Linda, 167

L
Lamb's Creek, 126
Lamb's Creek Church, 112, 113
Lampton, Hester Davis, 35
Lane, Henry, 68
Lane, Joseph, 68
Lauderdale, 105
Leake, George, 58
Lee, Andrew Maurice, 76
Lee, Ann, 83
Lee, B. N., 72
Lee, Baldwin, 69
Lee, Christine, 132
Lee, Galen, 132
Lee, George Thomas, 68
Lee, Harry Elgin, 77
Lee, Inez, 128
Lee, J., 72
Lee, James, 68
Lee, John, 136
Lee, Joseph F., 68
Lee, Keith, 136
Lee, Mrs., 58

Lee, Nellie, 128
Lee, Richard, 83
Lee, Richard Henry, 37, 161
Lee, Robert E., 89
Lee, T. Eldred, Jr., 75, 76
Lee, Thomas E., 29
Lee, Thomas Ludwell, 161
Leedstown Resolutions, 161
Legg, H., 60
Leitch, Chuck, 28
Lewis, Betty Washington, 80
Lewis, Daingerfield, 99
Lewis, Surg. G. W., 72
Lewis, George W., 68
Lewis, Henry B., 68
Lewis, Henry Byrd, 99
Lewis, James C., 147
Lewis, John C., 147
Lewis, Mabel Clift, 128
Lewis, W. B., 60
Lewis Egerton Smoot Library, 29
Liberty, 89
Lighthorse Henry Lee, 147
lightship, 146
Litchfield, 87, 88
Little Ark, 126, 127
Little Ark Baptist Church, 116, 118
Little Ferry Landing, 148
Little Zion, 115
Little, Cornelius, 77
Locust Dale, 104
Lomax, Thomas, 108
Lord Culpeper, 84
Lothian, 101
Lower Cedar Point, 146
Lucas, Lydia, 40
Lumpkin, Faye W., 22
Lunsford, J. L., 72
Lurty, John, 67

M
Machodoc Creek, 146, 148, 149, 150, 155
Machodoc Run, 156
Madison, Cleveland, 77
Madison, President James, 34, 35, 97, 152
Madison School, 127
Mann, Senator Paul, 167
Marders, Annie Bowler, 128
Marders, J., 72
Marders, Mrs., 58
Marengo, 38, 94, 116
Marlborough, 144
Marmaduke, John, 142
Marmeduke, Winter, 23
Marmion, 80, 82
Marshall, F. M., 60
Marshall, James, 67
Marshall, W., 60
Martin, J., 71
Mary (schooner), 150
Maryland Point, 146
Mason, Brooke, 136
Mason, Charles, 104
Mason, Charles V., 22
Mason, Elwood, 27, 136
Mason, George, 37
Mason, Jack, 27
Mason, John E.
Mason, Judge John E., 23, 103
Mason, Lawrence B., 25
Mason, Lawrence B., Jr., 26
Mason, Maria J. C., 119

Mason, Nicholas "Nick," 77
Mason, Walter, 165
Mason, Wily Roy, 106
Mason's Mill, 51
Massey, Thomas S. D., 68
Matanno, 144
Mathias Point, 145, 146, 147
Mathias Point School, 127
Mattacunt, 14
Mazingo, J., 71
McClanahan, G., 71
McClanahan, J. G., 72
McClanahan, William E., 69
McClanhan, J. H., 60
McDaniel, Billy, 23
McDaniel, Daniel, 69
McDaniel, George, 68
McDaniel, J., 72
McDaniel, John, 63
McDaniel, Thornton, 53
McDaniel, Virginia, 56
McGee, Charlie, 28
McGinniss, Helen, 128
McGinniss, Jack, 132
McGinniss, Richard, 128
McKenney, G., 60
McKenney, George B., 69
McKenney, William A., 23
McMaria Bluff, 149
McNabb, John, 23
Meade, Walter, 136
Merryman, Arthur, 77
Methodist Church, South, 122
Metomkin Point, 147
Metompkin Point, 145
Metropolitan Museum of Art, 82
Middleboro, 109
Miffleton, Daniel, 46
Miffleton, Webb, 23
Military Reconstruction Act, 73
Millbank, 98, 99, 151
Millbank Creek, 13
Miller, Luther, 63
Millville, 149
Minor, John, 68, 95
Minor, Wyatt, 55
Minter, Joe, 136
Mitchell, Lewis A., 77
Monchein, 107
Monroe, James, 36, 38, 41
Monroe, Spence, 36, 41
Monroe Mill, 149
Mont Chen, 107
Montague Baptist Church, 119, 121
Montague, Howard W., 116
Monte pier, 165
Monteith, Jesse J., 75
Monteith, N., 72
Montgomery, Sarah, 51
Moomaw, Gilbert, 26
Moore, Alice Campbell, 22
Moore, George, 53
Moore, Ida Green, 156
Moore, John, 151
Moore, R., 72
Moore, R. Walton, 162
Moreland, 83
Morengo, 93
Morgan, James R. "Happy", 55
Morgan, L., 60
Morgan, L. V., 60
Morgan, Sandford, 69
Morgan, Sanford, 23
Morgan, Winfield, 65

173

Morgantown Bridge, 162
Morris, Elmer, Jr., 55, 136
Morris, Elmer, Sr., 55
Morris, Junior, 40
Morris Chevrolet, 64
Moss, James, 68
Moss, Thornton, 68
Mothershead, Howard, 114
Mothershead, Robert, 102
Mothershead, Russell, 114, 136
Motley, John, 28
Mountain View, 103, 119
Mount Bethel Baptist Association, 31
Mount Chene, 107
Mount Ida, 101
Mount Mariah, 93, 105, 142
Mount Pleasant, 51, 105, 106
Mount Rose Canning Company, 26, 65
Mount Stuart, 86, 107
Mount Vernon, 109
Mt. Carmel Baptist Church, 119, 120
Muddy Creek, 19
Muddy Creek Church, 112
"Mule Hill," 80
Mullen, Mr., 58
Murphy, Lelia, 128
Muse, Lloyd, 63

N
Nalle, Elizabeth Wallace, 103
Nanzatico, 14, 96, 151, 152
Nanzemond Town, 13
Nanzemund Town, 13
Nash, J., 60
Nash, James, 144–145
Nash, John, 77
Naval Proving Ground, 57, 59, 148
Naval Proving Ground Railroad, 159
Neill, 147
Neill Post Office, 63
Neukam, Henry, 77
Newton, Jay, 28
Newton, L., 60
Newton, T., 60
Newton, Wallace, 65
Newton, Wayne, 12
Ninde, Dr. F. F., 23, 109
Norcum, 105
Norman Hill, 127
Norris, Frances, 128
Norris, Margaret, 128
Northern Neck Transportation, 24
Nuckols, Betty, 58
Nuckols, William, 136

O
O'Conor, Herbert R., 162
Oak Crest Vineyard and Winery, 64
Oaken Brow, 96
Oaken Brow Farm, 48
Oakland, 105
Oakland Baptist Church, 119
Office Hall, 38, 108
Ogle, Anne, 101
Ogle, Benjamin, 101
Olive, Annie Peyton, 62
Olive, Audrey, 128
Olive, Chester, 137
Osso, 95
Owens, 31

Owens, Barbara, 132
Owens, Bennie, 75
Owens, J., 60, 72
Owens, Kate, 135
Owens, Nannie, 62
Owens, Richard Henry, 61
Owens, Stanley, 132
Owens, W., 71
Owens, William, 68
Owens, William Windsor, 119
Owens Post Office, 62
Oyster Shell Landing, 148
Oyster Wars, 142
Ozatawomen, 14

P
Paddy, Nancy, 132
Padgett, Irvin, 62
Panorama, 47, 108
Parker, J., 60
Parker, Mrs. Peyton, 29
Parker, Shirley, 132
Parker's Store, 54
Parsons, Lt. Cdr. T. S., 60
Passapatanzy Creek, 143
Passapatanzy School, 126
Patawomeck tribe, 12
Patterson, Macon, 136
Pawnee (steamer), 145
Payne, Chastine, 23
Payne, Thomas, 105
Payne, William Gordon, 77
Peace and Light School, 129
Peace Lutheran Church, 123
Pecks, 101
Peed, J., 72
Peed, James Oscar, 70
Peed, John Nathaniel, 70
Peed, T. M., 72
Pemberton, W., 72
Peoples Union Baptist Church, 119, 121
Pepper Mill Creek, 159
Pepper Mill hill, 157
Perkins, Ens. F. M., 60
Perry, Harrison, 75
Perry, Mrs., 58
Perry, William M., 77
Persimmon Point, 145, 147
Peters, C. B., 60
Peyton, Carolinus, 40
Peyton, Charles, 58, 136
Peyton, Frank H., 63
Peyton, Robert Carter, 77
Peyton, Wesley, 40
Philipchuk, Ltjg. V., 60
Phillips, Coach, 136
Phillips, P., 71
Pierce, Isabella, 102
Pierce, Robert, 102
Pilgrim Church, 117
Pinker, Lt., 58
Pissaseck, 13
Pitts, Andrew, 145
Pitts, Dangerfield, 69
Pitts, Eleanor, 128
Pitts, Frank, 128
Pitts, Richard, 69
Pitts, Thomas, 128
Planter (vessel), 150
Pollard, John, 36
Pollard, P., 72
Pop Castle, 105
Popes Creek, Maryland, 147

Port Conway, 98, 150, 152
Port Royal, 150
Porter, A. Broaddus, 68
Portner, B.,
Portner, Farris, 26
Posey, Mr., 58
post offices, 62
Potomac (steamer), 151
Potomac Baptist Church, 118
Potomac Creek, 139
Potomac Elementary School, 129
Potomac Flotilla, 145
Potomac River, 140, 156
Potomac River Bridge, 54, 147, 152, 157, 16
Potts, W. W., 71
Pound, Bruce, 147
Powell, Jay, 42
Powhatan, 100, 101
Powhatan tribe, 12
Pratt, Cpl. J. H., 72
Pratt, William L., 142
Presidential Lakes, 106, 107
Preston Lodge No. 86, 30, 31
Price, Benjamin F., 68
Price, George W., 23
Price, James B., 142
Prim, 126
Prior, James Henry, 77
Providence Methodist Church, 122
Pullen, Joseph A., 23
Pulliam, E., 60
Purkins, Henry C., 23
Purkins, R. S., 72
Purkins, Richard Thomas, 23
Purkins, Thomas, 49, 105
Purks, Charles T., 54
Purks, Emerson, 40
Pursley, O., 72

Q
Quesenberry, Rose, 43
Quesenberry, Rousby P., 57
Quesenberry, William O., 75
Quisenberry, James, 102
Quisenberry, James S., 73

R
"Racket Hall," 96
Rakes, Buram D., 77
Ralph Bunche High School, 31, 134, 137
Ralph Bunche Student Store, 134
Rappahannock, 145, 152
Rappahannock River, 150, 152
Rappahannock River Valley National Wildlife Refuge, 52, 152
Rappahannocks, 13
Ratcliffe, 31
Ratcliffe, Cleveland K., 75
Rawlett, James, 68
Rawlett, Julian, 114
Rawlett, William, 68
Rawlette, J. B., 60
Reamy, Alexander, 61
Reamy, Bertha P., 61
Redman, J., 71
Redman, John A., 142
Redman, Silas, 41
Reeves, R., 60
Reno pier, 165
Revercomb, Hal, 136
Revercomb, Judge Horace A., Jr., 24

Revercomb Building, 24
Rice, R., 60
Rice, Samuel B., 116
Richardson, Ann, 167
Rigg, Benjamin, 67
Rigg, Betsey, 67
Riverside, Maryland, 147
Riverview, 127
Robb, John P., 68
Robinson, Sam, 26
Robinson, Sammy, 26
Robinson, William, 21
Rock, Raymond, 42
Rogers, A. A., 60
Rogers, Charlie, 128
Rogers, Frances, 128
Rogers, H., 72
Rogers, Hosea, 67
Rogers, W., 72
Rogers, W. E., 71
Rogers, William J., 23
Rokeby, 73, 103
Rokeby School, 129
Rollet, Jessie W., 68
"Rolling Light", 146
Rollins, Betty, 128
Rollins, Butler R., 75
Rollins, H., 68
Rollins, Lt. J., 72
Rollins, James, 128
Rollins, Lew, 58
Rollins, Samuel, 68
Rollins, William, 43, 74
Roosevelt, President Franklin D., 162
Rose, Alexander, 105
Rose, M., 60
Rose, Thomas, 68
Rose, W. A., 60
Rose, W. W., 68
Rose, William E., 68
Roseboom, Ltjg. J. H., 60
Rosenburg, Leon, 65
Rosenwald, Julius, 126
Rosier, John, 149
Rosier's Creek, 149
Rosier's Point, 149
Round Hill Baptist Church, 115, 116
Round Hill Episcopal Church, 112
Rowley, Frank, 114
Rowley, John, 14, 68

S
Salamone, Anthony, 77
Salem Baptist Church, 120
Samuel, Willie E., 77
Sanders, Mr., 58
Saunders, Virginia, 100
Scates, Sgt. James, 145
Scott, George W., 69
Scott, John Wesley, 77
Scott, Thomas, 68
Scrivener, C., 71
Seals, Anthony, 151
Sealston, 127, 151
Sealston Colored, 127
Sealston Elementary School, 130
Self, Mrs., 58
Shanklin, William, 116
Shaw, Gloria, 132
Shelbourne, 103
Shelley, Benjamin, 142
Shiloh, 127

Shiloh Baptist Church, 115, 116, 117, 122
Shiloh School, 131, 132
Shiloh Store, 54
Shirley, Henry G., 162
Shook, C., 60
Short, John, 80
Sisson, Dale W., 22
Sittenborne Parish, 111
Sixth Lord of Fairfax, 15
Skinker, John, 36
Skinker, Samuel, 151
Slocum, William K., 147
Smith, Capt. John, 11, 12, 14, 140
Smith, Mr., 136
Smith, Nicholas, 21
Smith, Susan, 106
Smith, Thomas, 38
Smith, William "Extra Billy", 38, 94
Smith, William Taylor, 106, 109
Smith's Wharf, 143
Smoot, Ann Hopewell, 29, 144
Smoot, Betty McGuire, 74
Smoot, Lewis, 85
Smoot, Lewis A., 144
Smoot, Mary, 147
Smoot, Richard, 147
Society Hill, 109
Somerset Beach, 143, 144
Sorrel, Zola, 58
Sorrell, James E., 77
Sperano, N., 60
Spicer, John, 21
Spilman, J., 72
Spilman, J. M., 72
Spring Hill, 38, 104
Spy Hill, 40, 46, 92, 93, 116, 148, 149
St. Anthony's Church, 123
St. Cloud, 105
St. John's Church, 112
St. Leger, 99
St. Paul's Church, 34, 87, 145, 156
St. Paul's Parish, 111, 112
St. Stephen's Baptist Church, 119, 120
Staples, Doris, 132
Staples, F., 60
Staples, F. B., 60
Staples, John L., 69
Staples, Newton, 75
Staples, S., 72
Staples, W. 72
Stephens, Betty, 132
Stephens, Jerry, 132
Stephens, Kenneth, 132
Steppe, Thomas, 53
Stewart, T., 60
Stiff, Andrew S., 69
Stiff's Wharf, 143
Stith, John, 89
Stokes, M., 72
Stone, Charles, 147
Stone, D., 60
Stony Point, 93
Storke, Dwight, 167
Strawberry Hill, 95
Strother, Ashby, 169
Strother, Edna, 58, 128
Strother, James, 69
Strother, Joseph, 21
Strother Church, 34
Strother family, 99
Strother's Church, 113

Stuart, Caroline Homoselle, 89
Stuart, David, 87, 112
Stuart, Hugh Roy, 148
Stuart, James Edward, 16
Stuart, John Hill, 86
Stuart, John, 89
Stuart, Margaret Robinson, 108
Stuart, Richard, 108
Stuart, Dr. Richard Henry, 43, 89, 108
Stuart, William, 87
Stuart family, 143
Stuart's Wharf, 143
Sullivan, Bernice, 58
Sullivan, William, 68
Sumner, Allen M., 75
Sumner Post No. 89, 31
Sunnyfield, 104
Suttle, Joe, 61
Suttle, Robert, 23
Suttles, J., 72

T
Taliaferro, James G., 128
Taliaferro, Col. John, 36
Taliaferro, Mary, 36
Tayloe, Capt. B. T., 68, 72
Tayloe, E. P., 68
Tayloe, Edward Thornton, 101
Tayloe, John, 48, 82, 101
Tayloe, William, 68
Taylor, Charles, 96
Taylor, Ed, 65
Taylor, M. O., 72
Taylor, Major, 69
Taylor, W. Robertson, 69
Taylor, Will, 30
Taylor, William B., 68
Taylor family, 103
Tennant, Alexander W., 68
Tennant's, Mr., 146
Tetotum, 40, 127, 149
Thebadour, Dennis, 132
Thomas, Fifth Baron of Cameron, 15
Thomas, Second Lord Culpeper, 15
Thomas, Sixth Lord Fairfax, 84
Thomas Baldwin Harris and Son, 54
Thomas Freeborn (steamer), 145
Thompson, Sgt. J. E., 72
Thompson, Preston, 136
Thompson, Steve, 136
Thompson, W., 72
Thornhill, D., 60
Thornley, William, 21
Thornton, Francis, 109, 148
Thornton, Col. Francis, 109
"Tick's Hole," 145
Tilp, Frederick, 145
Toby's Point, 52, 152
"Tompkin Point," 145
Toppahanocks, 13
Townshend, Richard, 94
Townshend, Robert, 94
Tricker, J., 72
Tricker, L., 72
Tricker, R., 72
Tricker, T., 72
Trigger, Katie Pitts, 128
Trinity Methodist Church, 122
Truman, President Harry S., 12
Truslow, Benjamin, 68
Tucker, Sarah, 83, 84
Turberville, Edward, 22

Turner, Caroline Matilda, 105
Turner, Carolinus, 96
Turner, George, 96
Turner, Harry, 25
Turner, Richard, 97, 109
Turner, Susan Rose, 39
Turner, Thomas, 25, 50
Turner family, 97
Two Rivers Baptist Church, 119
Tyson, John, 68

U
Underwood, Lawrence, 68
Union Bethel Baptist Church, 119
Union Methodist Church, 115, 122
Upper Cedar Point, 146

V
VanValzah family, 80
Virginia Department of Game and Inland Fisheries' Land's End Wildlife Management Area, 152
Virginia Plan, 35
Virginia Wine, 132
Vivian Hannah (sternwheeler), 154, 155
Vulcan Brick Company, 51

W
Wakefield (steamer), 147
Walker, Robert, 49
Wall, N., 60
Wallace, Arthur W., 75
Wallace, Gustavus, 103
Wallace, Michael, 94
Walsingham, 97, 109, 152
Ward, Captain James Harman, 145
Warren, W., 71
Washington, 149
Washington, Amelia Jane, 86
Washington, Augustine, 33, 48
Washington, Booker T., 126
Washington, Elizabeth, 100
Washington, George, 33, 48, 88, 94, 100, 141, 147, 148
Washington, Henry Thacker, 51
Washington, Henry Thacker, Jr., 82
Washington, John, 50, 67, 94, 144
Washington, Joseph E., 77
Washington, Lawrence, 50
Washington, Mary D., 146
Washington, Putnam S., 93
Washington, Tom, 58
Washington, Willis, 116
Washington family, 143
Washington Mill, 149, 150
Washington Parish, 112
Washington's Mill, 50
Wasner, A., 60
Waterloo, 94
Watts, Bob, 28
Watts, Mr., 114
Watts Mill, 149
Waugh, Mary, 38
Waugh Point, 140
Waverley, 40, 70, 108
Wayside Park, 31, 152
Weaver, Benjamin, 23
Weedon, Billie, 76
Weedon, Billie H., 46
Weedon, Billie T., 46
Weedon, Emma Rawlett, 76
Weedon, Thomas, 76
Weedon, Tommy, 46

Weedon's Mill, 149
Weedonville store, 54
Wegner, B., 60
Welch, Willie, 23
Welch family, 102
Welcome, 126, 127
Welcome Colored, 127
Weldon store, 54
Westmoreland Association, 161
Wheat, Dick, 26
Whipsawassen Creek, 140
White Hall, 94
White Plains, 102
White, A. G., 60
White, J., 60
White, J. F., 60
White, Mrs., 58
Whitman, Major Ezra, 162
Wickham, Senator Henry T., 162
Wiles, Mark Briton, 75
Wilkerson, D., 72
Wilkerson, Haynes, 26
Wilkerson, Joseph A., 69
Wilkins, Earl, 58
Wilkins, Raymond, 58
Wilkins, T. F., 58
Wilkinson, Newton, 68
Will Post Office, 63
Willard, Capt. Darwin, 72
Williams, Betty, 58
Williams, E. B., 60
Williams, Elsie H. S., 132
Williams, Cdr. G. K., 60
Williams, H. W. B., 65
Williams, William W., 77
Williams Creek Bridge, 157
Willow Hill, 73, 107, 130
Wilmont, 52, 150, 152, 153
Wilmont Fire Proofing Company, 51
Wilmont Wharf, 151
Windsor, 50, 92, 127
Windsor School, 127
Winston, Mrs. Olive, 126
Wishart, James, 94
Wolf, Peter, 23
Wolfe, C. Steven, II, 22
Woodford, William, 37
Wood Grove, 96
Woodlawn, 97, 109, 151
Woodlawn Historic and Archaeological District, 152
Woodstock, 89
Worrell, Ed, 60
Worrell, H., 72
Worrell, Henry, 68
Worrell, Hezekiah, 23
Worrell, Malcolm, 75
Worrell, W. W., 72
Worrell, Warren W., 72
Wren, Rosa, 96
Wroten, Margaret, 132
Wroten, Mazie, 132

Y
Yates Bar, 146
Yates Point, 147
Yellow Hill, 127

Z
Zion, Shiloh Meeting House, 114
Zorn, Gertrude, 58

About the Authors

— ELIZABETH NUCKOLS LEE —

Elizabeth Lee graduated from King George High School in 1964 and Mary Washington College in 1973. Until her retirement in 1994, she was employed at the Naval Surface Warfare Center. Since retiring, she has compiled and written several books about King George County court records and has published articles in the *Virginia Genealogical Society Magazine* and the *Northern Neck of Virginia Magazine of History*. She is a past member of the Virginia Genealogical Society Board of Directors, past president and member of the Friends of the Virginia State Archives Board of Directors, and past member of the Central Rappahannock Heritage Center Board of Directors. She is the current president of the King George County Historical Society and spends several days a week volunteering at the museum and researching in the courthouse.

She and her husband of forty-one years live in King George County, where they raised their four children. They are now enjoying being grandparents.

The King George County Historical Society and Museum are her passions. "Working with Jean Graham for the last ten years has been rewarding. It is an honor for me to share this endeavor with her."

— JEAN MARIE MOORE GRAHAM —

Jean fell in love with King George County when she moved to her grandfather's farm in the Machodoc Creek area when she was nine years old. After spending several years in King George, her family moved to the Washington, D.C., area, where she lived until 1988. During that time, she raised a family and worked for fourteen years with the Maryland school system. She earned an associate's degree in art in 1986. Jean and her husband of forty-eight years live in King George, the county of her roots, where they enjoy a beautiful view of the Potomac River.

After joining the King George County Historical Society in 1996, Jean became a dedicated volunteer in the King George County Museum & Research Center, spending at least one day a week at the museum. She loves research and genealogy and has spent numerous hours updating her King George County family tree. She is the editor of the King George County Historical Society's quarterly newsletter and enjoys researching new areas of the county's history. For the last few years, she has designed the historical society's entry for the Fall Festival Parade. She has also designed several of the society's annual brass ornaments. Jean states, "Working with Elizabeth in compiling this pictorial history has been an exciting task and a dream fulfilled."